Canada's Dream Shall Be of Them

CANADA'S DREAM SHALL BE OF THEM

Canadian Epitaphs of the Great War

ERIC MCGEER & STEVE DOUGLAS

WILFRID LAURIER
UNIVERSITY PRESS
www.wlupress.wlu.ca

Wilfrid Laurier University Press acknowledges the support of the Canada Council for the Arts for our publishing program. We acknowledge the financial support of the Government of Canada through the Canada Book Fund for our publishing activities. This work was supported by the Research Support Fund.

Library and Archives Canada Cataloguing in Publication

McGeer, Eric, author
   Canada's dream shall be of them : Canadian epitaphs of the Great War / Eric McGeer ; with photographs by Steve Douglas.

Includes bibliographical references.
Issued in print and electronic formats.
ISBN 978-1-77112-310-5 (hardcover).—ISBN 978-1-77112-311-2 (PDF).—ISBN 978-1-77112-312-9 (EPUB)

1. Epitaphs—Canada. 2. World War, 1914–1918—Casualties—Canada. 3. Cemeteries—France. 4. Cemeteries—Belgium—Flanders.
I. Douglas, Steve, 1956–, photographer II. Title. III. Title: Canadian epitaphs of the Great War.

| D639.D4M44 2017 | 940.4'6571 | C2017-901933-3 |
| | | C2017-901934-1 |

Front-cover photo by Steve Douglas. Cover design by Ryan Gearing. Interior design by Felicity Price-Smith.

Contents

Foreword

Much of the world remembers the First World War as a time when "innocent young men, their heads full of high abstractions like Honour and Glory … were slaughtered in stupid battles planned by stupid generals." English-speaking Canadians, while generally accepting this view, have supplemented it with a version of the war in which their soldiers won great victories and forged a new national identity on the slopes of Vimy Ridge. Both of these approaches have served to promote political and cultural agendas of such power that empirical studies of the experience of those who fought in the war and their families have had little impact upon the memory of the war.

Eric McGeer and Steve Douglas have both sought to understand an important aspect of the war's meaning by documenting the ways in which the families of those who died on the Great War battlefields choose to commemorate their loved ones. Their memory of the war was sharp and immediate, so when the next of kin were given the opportunity to select or compose an epitaph there was a wide range of responses. Many of the most moving are reproduced in this book.

Those of us who have visited the cemeteries maintained by the Commonwealth War Graves Commission have long been aware of the contrast between the ugliness of war and the tranquil beauty of the graveyards where our soldiers are buried. There is no irony to be found in the story of the creation of these places. To a large degree they are the vision of a man, Fabian Ware, who commanded a mobile unit of the Red Cross striving to save the wounded and record the temporary burial places of the dead. Ware knew that both tasks were of crucial importance to the soldiers who survived, each of whom feared that he might be left behind wounded or dead and forgotten. In the spring of 1917, the Committee for the Care of Soldiers Graves that Ware had created was transferred to the Imperial (later Commonwealth) War Graves Commission. The Canadian delegation attending the Imperial Conference of 1917 willingly agreed to participate in the work, contributing to the costs in proportion to the number of Canadian graves.

The decision to use a uniform style of headstone, normally of white Portland stone, and to make no distinction as to military or civilian rank, was followed by embracing the idea of encouraging families to be directly involved in selecting an epitaph with personal meaning. The cemeteries themselves were to follow a basic pattern with a Cross of Sacrifice and a Stone of Remembrance, but young architects who had served in the war were asked to design each cemetery. Eric McGeer and Steve Douglas have allowed us to join them in commemorating the war generation by developing a more informed memory of their sacrifice.

Terry Copp, March 2017

Introduction

Hidden in plain sight, throughout the hundreds of Commonwealth war cemeteries mapping the old Western Front, is a record unique to Britain and the Dominions of the old British Empire, that translates the human tragedy of the First World War from dulling numbers into poignant instances of the lives it consumed and the lives it despoiled. Thousands of personal inscriptions carved into the headstones of the fallen preserve the voice of the bereaved and enlist our sympathy, not only for those who died so young but for the next of kin who bore the burden of loss for the rest of their lives. The passage of time and the consolatory themes echoed in these messages of farewell may have eased this burden, but for an untold many the yearning grew with the days and years.

The most touching example of the war's lasting effect that I have ever seen took the form of a rough wooden plaque inserted beside the headstone of Sergeant Tom Holmshaw of the Royal Engineers, who died of wounds in June of 1917. Nearly eighty years later, his daughter made the journey to Lapugnoy War Cemetery to lay a token of remembrance at the grave of a father whose absence she felt all the more wistfully in the twilight of her own life: "You left me, dear father, when I was three … now aged 81 I have travelled and seen your resting place since 1917." Set alongside the words on her father's headstone, "Deeply missed by all who knew him," her offering is but one reminder that with each life lost in the Great War, a cherished part of many others also came to an end or, in the case of countless children, never began. Historians have long wrestled with the complexities of the Great War, its causes and consequences, yet one wonders if widowed mothers faced the harder task in explaining to uncomprehending children where their father had gone and why he would never return.

DEATH IS NOT A BARRIER TO LOVE, DADDY. KAYE
Private Peter William Lapointe MM, 2nd Battalion, August 17th 1918 (age 34)

OUR DEAR DADDY AND OUR HERO. WE MISS YOU.
Private George Sidney Brignell, 54th Battalion, September 20th 1918 (age 37)

NOTHING LEFT BUT BEAUTIFUL MEMORIES. HIS LOVING WIFE & BABY
Private Arthur Sillitoe, 13th Battalion, October 21st 1918 (age 21)

FOUGHT MANFULLY IN THE CAUSE, LEAVING MANY SAD HEARTS BEHIND HIM. MOTHER, WIFE, BABY
Lieutenant Louis Robert Maioni MC, Canadian Engineers, September 29th 1918 (age 29)

HE IS NOT DEAD WHOSE MEMORY STILL IS LIVING WITHIN A NATION'S HEART. WIFE & LITTLE SON
Major Norman Campbell Pilcher, 5th Canadian Mounted Rifles, May 19th 1916 (age 37)

DECEASED LEAVES ONE SON, DAVID LEONARD WHITE, BORN FEB. 12 1917.
Private Vance Smith White, 20th Battalion, October 12th 1918 (age 24)

THE LOVING HUSBAND OF EDITH BOWDITCH AND DARLING DADDY OF LITTLE VINNA. R.I.P.
Private Alfred George Bowditch, 8th Battalion, September 13th 1918 (age 31)

DEARLY LOVED HUSBAND OF JESSIE REEVE & DARLING DADDY OF LITTLE BILLY.
Company Sergeant Major Henry Reeve, 25th Battalion, September 25th 1918 (age 36)

DON, AS YEARS GO BY WE MISS YOU MORE. LOVING WIFE AND DAUGHTER GLADYS
Private Cecil Donald Shaw, 25th Battalion, February 6th 1916 (age 23)

TO-DAY AND YESTERDAY, BUT LESS THAN TOMORROW.
Gunner Norman Burgess, Canadian Field Artillery, September 22nd 1917 (age 37)

In memory of the Canadians who fought and died in the Great War, and the families devastated by their loss, this book takes for its subject the personal inscriptions found on the headstones of Canadian soldiers at rest in France and Flanders. It gathers into one place a representative selection of about a thousand examples drawn from a wide array of war cemeteries, some on the beaten track, others sequestered in remote areas all the more worth seeking out for their solitude and silence. My purpose is to present these epitaphs in such a way as to illuminate the response of the Canadian populace, individually and collectively, to the conflicting legacy of the Great War. What that legacy was can be gleaned from the six words on the grave of Private Richard Vidal, killed ten weeks before the Armistice: "Victory, but the price was dear." The legendary performance of the Canadian Expeditionary Force and the decisive part that Canadian soldiers played in achieving the victory brought renown to a hitherto obscure Dominion of the British Empire and remain a source of national pride to this day. But the war also claimed over 65,000 Canadian lives and left another 170,000 wounded, crippled, or broken in mind. The epitaphs reconnect us with the emotions, reactions, and attitudes of the people left in the immediate aftermath of the Great War to confront this loss, to make sense of what had happened, and to honour a debt of remembrance to those who had sacrificed themselves for a cause that English Canadians, if not their French-speaking *concitoyens*, had believed to be just and righteous and necessary.

Courcelette British Cemetery, in the heart of the Somme battlefields, contains nearly 2,000 graves, including 783 Canadians laid to rest alongside their British and Australian comrades in arms.

FOUR YEARS HAVE PASSED AND STILL I MISS HIM. HOW I MISS HIM NONE CAN TELL. MOTHER
Private George Hall, 60th Battalion, April 3rd 1917 (age 35)

BORN AT HUMBER BAY, CANADA, NOV. 25 1884. OF 74TH BN. FROM TORONTO, SPRING 1916.
Private Septimus Herbert Hicks, 42nd Battalion, August 6th 1916 (age 31)

BREAK, DAY OF GOD, SWEET DAY OF PEACE, AND BID THE SHOUT OF WARRIORS CEASE.
Sergeant Wellesley Seymour Taylor, 14th Battalion, May 1st 1916 (age 24)

TO YOU FROM FAILING HANDS WE THROW THE TORCH; BE YOURS TO HOLD IT HIGH.
Corporal Harry Leggo Hammond, Princess Patricia's Canadian Light Infantry, September 30th 1918 (age 22)

ONE OF CANADA'S GIFTS TO THE EMPIRE, A LIFE.
Private William Smith, 49th Battalion, September 29th 1918 (age 24)

GOD SAID, "THE FIRST BORN OF THY SONS SHALT THOU GIVE UNTO ME."
Lance Corporal Norman McKelvie Parker, 58th Battalion, September 26th 1917 (age 20)
[Exodus 22:29]

The process by which the Imperial War Graves Commission came to allow personal inscriptions on the headstones, the rules applying, and the general characteristics and themes of the epitaphs are discussed in the second chapter. For the moment, however, some preliminary observations will help to shape the approaches to the subject. It is important, first of all, to note that the epitaphs were composed (or selected) in the years immediately after the war, in the early 1920s, when hopes that the sacrifice would lead to a better world, to concord between nations, to an end of war had not yet given way to the disillusionment, contrition, and rejection of the war's justification that emerged later in the decade and hardened in the 1930s. A canon of commemorative verse and formulae, exemplified by Laurence Binyon's "For the Fallen," John Arkwright's "O Valiant Hearts," and, dear to Canadians, John McCrae's "In Flanders Fields," had also taken shape during the war and influenced the themes and diction of valedictory inscriptions. We should bear in mind, too, that the epitaphs commemorate soldiers born in the 1880s and 1890s to parents born between the 1850s and 1870s and hence steeped in the confident culture, traditions, and certainties of the Victorian age – from which, as Jay Winter has rightly argued, the war did not dislodge them. The epitaphs, in short, offer a Victorian response to a twentieth-century disaster. They were contributed not by the poets or artists we tend to associate with the Great War and modern memory, but by ordinary men and women predominantly British in background and outlook, whether they were born in Canada or Great Britain, who worshipped the stern, punitive Jehovah of the Old Testament and the sacrificial, redemptive Jesus of the New; who believed that progress came at a price; and who had a far higher pain threshold, physically and mentally, than we do. They had to. Open any newspaper or magazine of the time, and what leaps out is the number of advertisements hailing quack cures and remedies for the aches, complaints, conditions, and assorted ailments that they put up with and that modern medicine has long since expunged from our lives. In a day and age before penicillin, antibiotics, insulin, or the polio vaccine, when childbirth was still fraught with risk, and random illnesses and accidents carried off young and old alike, suddenly and indiscriminately, life in pre-1914 Canada was hard and precarious and non-negotiable, ripe with discomfort and best approached with a certain fatalism. On the other hand, it braced one for the rigours of trench warfare, and we may surmise that the harsher realities of their time went some way to inure people to the ordeal of the war.

All this is to say that reading the epitaphs of the Great War with modern sensibilities is to read them through a lens distorted by the march of time and the cultural shift wrought by the 1960s. They are a window into another world, not a mirror to our own. Irony, protest, or cynicism, reactions instinctive today, are exceedingly rare exceptions to the sincerity of the personal inscriptions of a hundred years ago. As we shall see, the War Graves Commission granted next of kin some leeway in the composition of the epitaphs, so that pointed submissions, within limits, were judged permissible. "He did his duty. My heart knoweth its own bitterness. Mother"; "A bursting bud on a slender stem, broken and wasted, our boy"; "Sacrificed to the fallacy that only war can end war." These striking British examples demonstrate the range of acceptable content and tone, but to rely once again on Jay Winter, the bereaved drew upon the tried and true reassurances of the traditional, rather than the modernist and experimental, to find comfort in their sorrow. Irony, protest, or cynicism give vent to anger or bitterness, but they prolong rather than pacify grief. "Yet stones have stood for a thousand years, and pained hearts found the honey peace in old poems" – beautifully crafted and wise, the closing lines of Robinson Jeffers's "To the Stone-cutters" (1925) offer the truest counsel by which to read the epitaphs of the Great War, as testaments to the fallen and their families' search, so human and so necessary, for the repose or release that would allow them, as best they could, to resume their lives.

WORDS FAIL OUR LOSS TO TELL.
Driver Reginald Frank Davey, Canadian Field Artillery, September 5th 1918 (age 25)

Some could not. This must also bear on our understanding of the epitaphs. In the University of Toronto archives is a letter from a Mr. A.K. Goodman to the university registrar then engaged in compiling a Roll of Honour of the 628 students killed on active service. Mr. Goodman's son, Lieutenant Ambrose Harold Goodman, had died of wounds after a heroic action in August of 1918. After giving the details of his son's death, Mr. Goodman went on to write that "Harold was a very wholesome boy, but 21, and excelled in the outdoor sports … his violin, banjo & piano which gave so much pleasure to his circle are silent. This intensifies our loss and being an only child made it very hard for me to let him go." Even though his son's sacrifice had ensured that "Right dominated Wrong," and despite his insistence that "we too must be of heroic mould tho' ours are the homes that mourn," these stoic words were of no avail. The Great War killed son and father. Mr. Goodman was dead within a year, having declined noticeably since receiving word of his son's death and losing his will to live, according to his obituary. How many bravely worded epitaphs likewise mask a desolation of grief that in the end was inexpressible and irremediable?

GONE. THERE IS NO OTHER. MOTHER
Private Richard Edward Symons, 102nd Battalion, May 1st 1918 (age 21)

AN ACTOR BY PROFESSION. HIS LAST ROLE, THE NOBLEST EVER PLAYED.
Private Griffith Tallesyn Davies, Canadian Army Medical Corps, May 20th 1918 (age 50)

METHODIST LOCAL PREACHER. UNIVERSITY STUDENT, TORONTO. MY BEST BOY.
Lieutenant George Dundas, MC and Bar, Royal Field Artillery, September 2nd 1918 (age 25)

ENGLISH CHANNEL

Nieuport

Ghent

Malines

Calais

Passchendaele

Ypres
Hill 62 –
St Eloi Mount Sorrel

BRUSSELS

St Omer

Lys

BELGIUM

Lille

Tournai

Nivelles

Festubert

Etaples

Bethune

Mons

Sambre

Hill 70

Vimy

Douai

Valenciennes

Dinant

Arras

Philippeville

Abbeville

Cambrai

Beaumont
Hamel Courcelette

FRANCE

Le Cateau

Albert

Canal du Nord

Somme

Blangy

Oise

Amiens

St Quentin

Grandvilliers

Serre

Montdidier

Signy l'Abbaye

N

Laon

Beauvais

Compiègne

Aisne

Meuse

Western Front, July 1916

0   5   10   25 miles

LATE ROYAL NORTH WEST MOUNTED POLICE, YUKON DIVISION.
Private Harry Lovell Simons, 29th Battalion, November 3rd 1915 (age 37)

SLEEP, DEAR SON. HONOUR, JUSTICE, DUTY, ALL SURVIVE BY YOUR MORTAL FALL.
Lieutenant Mackay Mackay, Princess Patricia's Canadian Light Infantry, August 27th 1918 (age 28)

WHEN THOU PASSEST THROUGH THE WATERS I WILL BE WITH THEE. PSA. LXIII
Lance Corporal William Henry McConnell, 85th Battalion, September 27th 1918 (age 29)

HIS LIFE WAS GENTLE THAT NATURE MIGHT SAY TO ALL THE WORLD, THIS WAS A MAN. (SHAKESPEARE)
Lieutenant Howard Taylor, 5th Battalion, June 6th 1916 (age 21)

MR. GREAT HEART. OFFICER AND GENTLEMAN.
Major William Henry Grant, 44th Battalion, October 25th 1916 (age 32)

A GIFTED SURGEON. KILLED AT THE POST OF DUTY. BELOVED BY ALL.
Captain Ethelbert Eldridge Meek, Canadian Army Medical Corps, May 30th 1918 (age 41)

KILLED IN ACTION. BELOVED DAUGHTER OF ANGUS & MARY MAUD MACDONALD, BRANTFORD, CANADA
Nursing Sister Katherine MacDonald, Canadian Army Nursing Service, May 19th 1918 (age 31)

ICI REPOSE LE CORPS DE PHILIPPE BAILLARGEON. TUÉ EN ACTION PAR LES BOMBES DES ALLEMANDS.
[HERE LIES THE BODY OF PHILIPPE BAILLARGEON. KILLED IN ACTION BY GERMAN BOMBS.]
Private Philippe Baillargeon, Canadian Army Medical Corps, May 30th 1918 (age 21)

ONE OF THE MANY CANADIAN INDIANS WHO DIED FOR THE EMPIRE.
Private Lawrence Marten, 52nd Battalion, October 5th 1916 (age 33)

HE WAS THE FIRST ICELANDER TO GIVE HIS LIFE FOR CANADA. I THANK YOU, MY SON.
Private Magdal Hermanson, 8th Battalion, May 3rd 1915 (age 19)

DANS LES MOMENTS CRITIQUES JE DISAIS TROIS FOIS "JE VOUS SALUE, MARIE."
[AT CRITICAL MOMENTS I WOULD REPEAT THREE TIMES, "HAIL, MARY."]
Lieutenant Pierre Eugène Guay, 22nd (French Canadian) Battalion, May 1st 1918 (age 24)

Opposite: Map of the Western Front marking the Canadian battlefields of the Great War.

ONLY SON OF ROBERT DONNAN, BALYCRAN, CO. DOWN, IRELAND.
KILLED NEAR LENS IN HIS FIRST ENGAGEMENT.
Private William Donnan, 46th Battalion, May 3rd 1917 (age 45)

A LOVER OF CHILDREN AND FLOWERS. A GOOD FRIEND AND PATRIOTIC.
Private John Delaney, 2nd Canadian Mounted Rifles, June 5th 1917 (age 37)

ETONENSIS OXONIENSIS. FILI, FRATER, MARITE, PATER, AVE ATQUE VALE CARISSIME.
[GRADUATE OF ETON AND OXFORD. DEAREST SON, BROTHER, HUSBAND, FATHER, HAIL AND FAREWELL.]
Private Kenneth Myers, 72nd Battalion, July 22nd 1918 (age 31)

LOVED ONES HE LEFT AND BABE UNBORN. SLEEP ON TILL RESURRECTION MORN.
Gunner Lambert Taylor, Canadian Field Artillery, August 26th 1917 (age 34)

LIKE A SOLDIER FELL FOR KING AND COUNTRY ON 18TH BIRTHDAY.
Private Roy Novello Riley, 13th Battalion, August 8th 1916 (age 18)

SERVED WITH HONOUR AND WAS DISABLED IN THE GREAT WAR.
Private James Singleton, Canadian Army Service Corps, February 3rd 1920 (age 31)

ALL WE HAD. LOVED AND DEEPLY MISSED BY FATHER AND MOTHER.
Private Albert Arthur Briggs, 2nd Battalion, April 26th 1916 (age 23)

THE ONLY CHILD OF AGED PARENTS.
Private Vernon Keith Merchant, 58th Battalion, June 6th 1916 (age 16)

"To see the world in a grain of sand …" One at a time the epitaphs coalesce into a remarkably varied register full of historical and human interest. They convey the meaning and consolation that the Great War generation sought in its distress, and the emotional force of its response to a tragedy of unprecedented scale. They retrieve, even if momentarily, the individuals caught up in the maelstrom of the Great War. They indicate the principal sources to which the mourners turned for solace and inspiration, the King James Version, *The Pilgrim's Progress*, or the classics of English literature; but they also show that many looked elsewhere or within themselves. More importantly, even though tending to idealize the fallen, a great many impart something of who the Glorious Dead really were, as human beings rather than as symbols – what set them apart, what they were to others, what made their fate so singular and sad

Opposite: A.Y. Jackson *Gas Attack, Lievin*
[CWM 19710261-0179 Beaverbrook Collection of War Art, Canadian War Museum]

to recall. It is strange, then, that only in the last twenty years or so have the personal inscriptions attracted the attention they deserve. John Laffin's collection of Australian epitaphs, *We Will Remember Them* (1995), and Trefor Jones's anthology of British and Dominion epitaphs, *On Fame's Eternal Camping Ground* (2007), are two valuable works that opened my eyes to the possibilities inherent in a book about Canadian epitaphs. Where my perspective is horizontal, looking at the broader themes and relevance of the epitaphs, others take a vertical approach. Sarah Wearne has lately published a well-chosen selection of personal inscriptions from the battle of the Somme (*Epitaphs of the Great War: The Somme*) in which she delves into the sources and meaning of each one and relates it to the soldier commemorated. A similarly presented collection of epitaphs from Passchendaele will be a most welcome companion volume, and she is providing a useful forum with her Great War Epitaphs (@wwinscriptions) and website (epitaphsofthegreatwar.com), which interested readers are strongly advised to visit. Her work is proof that the more researchers bring to the epitaphs, the more these gems of compression will have to say. It is therefore one purpose of this book, in conjunction with those cited above, to bring this fascinating body of material to a wider audience and to promote the integration of a largely untapped source into studies of the myth and memory of the Great War.

EVERY NOBLE LIFE LEAVES A FIBRE OF IT INTERWOVEN
FOR EVER IN THE WORK OF THE WORLD. RUSKIN
Lance Sergeant David Horne, 75th Battalion, March 1st 1917 (age 34)

Commenting in 1919 on the many and diverse works of art exhibited by the Canadian War Memorials Fund, the British art critic Paul Konody quoted the venerable John Ruskin's maxim that "great nations write their autobiographies in three manuscripts – the book of their deeds, the book of their words, and the book of their art," the last being the key to the other two. Whether Konody or Ruskin would have ranked the young Dominion of Canada among the great nations is a question for another day, but for our purposes the book of deeds was written by Canada's soldiers, the book of words by a populace in mourning, and the book of art by the painters whose works have been included here and by my colleague Steve Douglas, whose photographs portray the war cemeteries, the monuments, and the landscapes that connect the book of deeds with the book of words. It is our

La Plus Douve Farm Cemetery, south of Ypres (Ieper), contains 88 Canadian graves among its 345 burials.

hope that this book, an aggregate of these three elements, will inspire Canadians to visit the battlefields and war cemeteries where a significant portion of our history is preserved in perpetuity.

LEST WE FORGET HOW GREAT THE DEBT WE OWE TO THOSE WHO DIED.
Private James Atkinson, Canadian Army Medical Corps, June 15th 1918 (age 29)

The book has been written amidst a flurry of centenaries – Vimy Ridge and Passchendaele in 2017, Amiens and the Hundred Days in 2018 – which, along with those of Second Ypres (2015), Hill 62 and the Somme (2016) already observed, are the landmark events in the history and lore of Canada's Great War. Of these, Vimy Ridge looms largest in Canadian memory, and so the first chapter offers a reconsideration of this epic battle based on the epitaphs of the soldiers who lie at rest near the most impressive and most famous of Canada's war memorials. There follows a chapter on the personal inscriptions themselves, discussing their origins, themes, and sources, as well as their place in the national memory of the Great War, whereupon we return to the battlefields selected as the sites of official commemoration. The Brooding Soldier near St. Julien, and the memorial stones at Hill 62, Courcelette, Passchendaele, Le Quesnel, Dury, and Bourlon Wood have become stations on the Canadian pilgrimage route along the Western Front, just as the majestic caribou monument at Beaumont Hamel has become a shrine for Newfoundlanders and their fellow Canadians. In chapters on the Ypres Salient, the Somme, Passchendaele, and the Hundred Days, my aim has been to use the epitaphs as a means to reflect upon the human experience and cost of these battles, both to honour the men who fell and to remember the plight of their families. The final chapter consists of a list of epitaphs that allows readers simply to browse and cast their minds back to the most traumatic years in Canada's history. A hundred years later, we rightly pay tribute to the soldiers of the Canadian Corps who brought renown to their country, but the centenary of the Great War is also the occasion to give due recognition to the strength of character and common decency of men and women rarely mentioned in the history books, yet who bequeathed to later generations their own worthy legacy of courage and endurance.

ENLISTED WESTVILLE, PICTOU, NOVA SCOTIA, CANADA.
Private Joseph Richardson, 85th Battalion, September 30th 1918 (age 19)

BORN IN NOVA SCOTIA. KILLED AT THE BATTLE OF CAMBRAI.
Private Clarke John Wheaton, 25th Battalion, October 9th 1918 (age 20)

OF FALMOUTH, N.S. KILLED IN ACTION NEAR ARRAS FRONT.
Private James Cope, 25th Battalion, April 17th 1918 (age 19)

BORN MAY 1897 AT BURTT'S CORNER, YORK CO., N.B. DIED OF WOUNDS AGED 20.
Private Frederick William Inch, Princess Patricia's Canadian Light Infantry, November 12th 1917

CANADIEN FRANÇAIS. CATHOLIQUE. DE CHICOUTIMI, P.Q. R.I.P.
Private Joseph Jean, 52nd Battalion, June 6th 1916 (age 26)

BORN AT OTTAWA, ONTARIO. THE ROSE STILL GROWS BEYOND THE WALL.
Sapper Gordon Harper Bowie, Canadian Railway Troops, August 31st 1918 (age 22)

A TORONTO BOY. OUR ONLY SON. HE LOVED PEACE. FOR CANADA HE SERVED.
Sergeant George Fredrick Stone Hayden, Canadian Field Artillery, July 17th 1917 (age 26)

HOME COOKSTOWN, ONT. ENLISTED FROM FLEMING, SASK., CANADA.
Corporal George Elmer McMaster, Canadian Army Medical Corps, August 19th 1918 (age 30)

BORN AT BRAMPTON, ONT. ENLISTED MARCH, 1916, EDMONTON, ALTA.
Gunner Robert Godfrey Hunter, Canadian Field Artillery, 17.9.18 (age 28)

SON OF JAMES & HARRIET PROVEN, GLANWILLIAM, MANITOBA. SERVED 3 YEARS & 8 MONTHS.
Sergeant Harry James Proven, 1st Canadian Mounted Rifles, September 29th 1918 (age 25)

BORN AT PILOT MOUND, MANITOBA AND BROUGHT UP AT BATTLE CREEK, SASK.
Private Alexander Everett Parsonage, 1st Canadian Mounted Rifles, June 2nd 1916 (age 23)

DIED OF WOUNDS. ENLISTED AUG. 8 1914. SON OF W. P. SPARLING, CARNDUFF, SASK.
Private Howard Clarence Sparling, Canadian Army Service Corps, June 5th 1917 (age 24)

ENLISTED AUG. 12, 1914, MOOSIMIN, SASK., CANADA.
Lance Corporal Henry Chilton, 5th Battalion, June 3rd 1916 (age 34)

BORN JAN. 9TH 1897 IN MACLEOD, ALBERTA, CANADA. HE IS AT HOME & SAFE IN HEAVEN.
Private William Curtis Hewson, 27th Battalion, January 9th 1917 (age 20)

TWENTY YEARS, SEVEN MONTHS AND NINE DAYS. SON OF WILLIAM AND JANET MCALLISTER, EDMONTON.
Private Russell Scobie McAllister, 31st Battalion, April 6th 1918 (age 20)

ONLY SON OF VEN. ARCHDEACON SWEET, VICTORIA, B.C. A MAN GREATLY BELOVED.
Major John Hales Sweet, 72nd Battalion, April 9th 1917 (age 38)

A NATIVE OF NANAIMO, B.C. CANADA. ALL'S WELL, SONNY, ALL'S WELL.
Lieutenant Harold Sherratt Cunningham, 47th Battalion, August 16th 1918 (age 20)

A final word on the title of this book. "From little towns we came, by little towns we lie …" – Rudyard Kipling's brief elegy to Canada's fallen strikes a chord when one sees the placenames on their graves, linking them to homes from one end of the country to the other. Where British soldiers going on leave were less than a day's journey from home, and pilots on patrol over the battlefields could at times catch sight of England, Canadian soldiers could return to their homes only in thought. Did they dream of Canada, wondered the poet Helena Coleman (1860–1953) in her "Autumn 1917," a poem evoking the splendours of a Canadian fall, and did these dreams, tinged with memories of childhood, sustain them in a landscape ablaze with colours more ominous than any in nature? For the soldiers, then fighting for their lives at Passchendaele, she could not speak; but in her gratitude and remembrance of them she ventured a prophecy, in two beautiful, haunting lines, that parents in Priceville, Ontario, chose for their son's headstone in the war cemetery near the village of Aubigny-en-Artois. A century later it speaks for all the young men and women at rest far from their homes in the Maritimes, along the St. Lawrence and Great Lakes, across the Prairies, and beyond the Rockies, yet forever inscribed in the national memory of the Great War.

IN YEARS TO COME WHEN TIME IS OLDEN, CANADA'S DREAM SHALL BE OF THEM.
Gunner Donald Lachlan McKinnon, Canadian Field Artillery, September 17th 1917 (age 25)

Opposite: Alfred Bastien *Canadian Sentry, Moonlight, Neuville-Vitasse*
[CWM 19710261-0058 Beaverbrook Collection of War Art Canadian War Museum]

1

STORIED VIMY'S HILL

Vimy Ridge holds primacy of honour in Canada's memory of the Great War, and the ceremonies marking the battle's centenary will take pride of place in the commemorations honouring the achievements of the legendary Canadian Corps. The main ceremony at the Vimy Memorial will recall the great pilgrimage of 1936, when over six thousand Canadian veterans and bereaved next of kin crossed land and sea to witness King Edward VIII dedicate the most impressive monument on the old Western Front. It will furnish occasion once more to reflect upon the significance of Vimy Ridge, both as a feat of arms and the crucible of Canadian nationhood, and upon the trials of a generation of Canadians whose lives were ended, blighted, or forever altered by the First World War. Though that generation has long since served its day, its legacy and presence linger in the immaculately tended cemeteries spread about the landscape below the ridge. There, in the solemn quiet of isolated places, the courage of the battlefield stands revealed in the ordered rows of headstones. So, too, does another kind of courage, the courage to endure, in the moving, dignified farewells from the parents, wives, and children for whom the war never ended.

"He was a prince under fire."
"Faithful unto death."
Private Ernest Lloyd Edgley, 24th Battalion, April 9th 1917 (age 26)

Last words to his comrade, "Go on, I'll manage."
Private Ernest Albert Proven, 1st Canadian Mounted Rifles, April 12th 1917 (age 21)

In loving memory of our beloved sons who died for King and Country.
Private William James West, 14th Battalion, April 9th 1917 (age 19)
Private Arthur West, 14th Battalion, April 9th 1917 (age 27)

As with all pilgrimages, faith is the prime mover. There is much about Vimy that Canadians have taken on faith ever since the men who reached the crest put up their own memorials to the victory that they and their fallen comrades had won. That Vimy proved the prowess and skill of Canadian soldiers and forged the reputation of the Canadian Corps is beyond dispute; but it was not a uniquely Canadian battle, nor decisive, nor even the greatest Canadian victory of the war. That distinction Sir Arthur Currie reserved for the breaking of the Hindenburg Line in September of 1918, an operation for which the Corps had four days, not three months, to prepare, an assault into the most formidable defences the Canadians ever faced, and a costly success that sealed the outcome of the war. Second Ypres had revealed their raw courage, Hill 62 their resilience, Courcelette their determination, Passchendaele their fortitude, Amiens their enterprise, Dury and Bourlon Wood their resourcefulness. It was the aggregate of these qualities that made the Canadian Corps the most effective instrument in the British Expeditionary Force, if not the entire Allied coalition, during the war-winning offensives of 1918. Yet in Canadian memory, then as now, Vimy Ridge eclipsed these other battles and was selected as the site where Walter Allward's soaring allegory in stone would give expression to the country's grief for her faraway dead, and exalt the ends to which her soldiers had been the means.

TENDER THOUGHTS FROM A DISTANCE
Lance Sergeant Ernest Whitfield, 49th Battalion, April 9th 1917 (age 31)

COULD I BUT JUST HAVE CLASPED HIS HAND AND WHISPERED, MY SON, FAREWELL.
Private Sidney James Cope MM, Royal Canadian Regiment, April 9th 1917 (age 23)

THE BRAVE LIES FAR FROM HOME, HIS PARENTS' HEARTS MELTING WITH PAIN.
Private Clifford Doucet, Royal Canadian Regiment, April 11th 1917 (age 21)

SPIRIT IN HEAVEN, BODY IN FRANCE, MEMORY IN CANADA.
Private Earl Orrington MacKinnon, 10th Battalion, April 9th 1917 (age 19)

THE WORK OF RIGHTEOUSNESS SHALL BE PEACE.
Private Campbell MacAskill, Royal Canadian Regiment, April 9th 1917 (age 22)

FOR LIBERTY, TRUTH AND RIGHTEOUSNESS.
Private Grant Monroe Phelps, 1st Battalion, April 9th 1917 (age 28)

FOR FAITH AND LIBERTY.
Private Orton Griffin, 58th Battalion, April 12th 1917 (age 18)

HIS OWN WORDS, TO FIGHT FOR FREEDOM.
Private Earl Arthur Shelters, 1st Canadian Mounted Rifles, April 9th 1917 (age 21)

Georges Bertin Scott *Unveiling Vimy Ridge Monument*
[CWM 19670070-014, Beaverbrook Collection of War Art,
Canadian War Museum]

With the approach of the centenary in mind, historians revisiting the battle have subjected the received memory of Vimy Ridge to cross-examination and presented some necessary correctives to the rather lopsided Canadian version of events. They have reminded us that the Canadian Corps fought under British command, that the Canadian attack was but one part of a larger British offensive that carried on for a month after the capture of the ridge, that the meticulously planned and executed artillery barrage was the brainchild of British staff officers and the combined work of British, Australian, and Canadian gunners, that the 2nd Canadian Division was reinforced by two British battalions, and that, although much of the attack unfolded according to plan, there were places where things went badly wrong. Outstanding as it was, the Canadian success was curtailed by the intractable factor that hobbled all armies in the Great War – as soon as the infantry outdistanced its artillery support, the attack was over. Limited success meant limited impact, for even though the Canadians now controlled the feature dominating the front north of Arras, the depth and strength of the German defences reimposed the rigid stalemate that continued until the last months of the war.

It could also be argued that the real, if unforeseen, benefit of Vimy was to become apparent the following year, when Allied occupancy of the ridge helped stem the tide of the German offensives launched in March of 1918. Since the heavily fortified eminence was impregnable on the steeper eastern slope, the Germans avoided the area and diverted their attacks into two streams north and south of the sector held by the Canadian Corps. This gave the Canadians a precious respite from the fighting throughout the first half of 1918 and allowed them to replenish their ranks and prepare for the riposte that all knew must come once the enemy had exhausted his strength.

Right: The grave of Private Lewis Edgar West in Lapugnoy War Cemetery.
He was killed five months after his two brothers, Arthur and William James, fell at Vimy Ridge.
Opposite: A.Y. Jackson Vimy Ridge from Souchez Valley (Sketch)
[CWM 19710261-0172 Beaverbrook Collection of War Art Canadian War Museum]

When the moment came the Allied high command entrusted the task to a reinvigorated Corps primed to spearhead the great counterattack. Their performance in the Hundred Days campaign, the one time that Canada played a leading role on the world stage, hastened not just the final victory but the end of a seemingly endless war.

Reassessments of Vimy do not detract from the Canadian achievement, nor is that the intention behind them. They aim to dispel the myths that distort or sentimentalize our understanding of the battle, the young men who fought and died, and the people of a very different day and age. The convergence of two milestone anniversaries in 2017, the Vimy centenary and Canada's sesquicentennial, will enhance the patriotic glow over the commemorative ceremonies, but if Vimy Ridge is to be hailed as a nation-building event, we have a duty, out of fidelity to the past, to perceive the architects for what they were and the significance of their efforts and sacrifice as contemporaries did. The epitaphs commemorating the men killed at Vimy carry us back to the years following the Armistice when memories of the conflict were still vivid and its impact keenly felt. Beyond adding new or unexpected details to the story, a selection of the inscriptions from Vimy Ridge allows a generation far removed from the trauma of the Great War to see why the battle attained such iconic status in Canadian eyes, and which elements of the consoling vision that arose in response to the war's terrible exactions have survived the journey to the present.

A CANADIAN HERO.

Private Joseph Wallace Aitchison, 38th Battalion, April 11th 1917 (age 20)

The headstone of Captain William James Withrow in Ecoivres War Cemetery:
"A knight without fear and without reproach," he took command of the Topographical Section
and helped to develop the plans for the assault on Vimy Ridge. Exhausted from his work but
refusing to go on leave, he died of heart failure. He was 48 years old.

OF TORONTO, CANADA. DIED AT VIMY RIDGE. AT REST.
Private Sydney James Luck, Princess Patricia's Canadian Light Infantry, April 9th 1917 (age 27)

PRINCIPAL, PUBLIC SCHOOLS, ARMSTRONG, B.C. VIMY RIDGE. O VALIANT HEART.
Private Thomas Rankine, 46th Battalion, April 16th 1917 (age 40)

FOR ENGLAND, HOME AND DUTY, AND THE HONOUR OF HIS RACE.
Lance Corporal Arthur Walter Lake, 54th Battalion, April 10th 1917 (age 30)

SCOTCH SOLICITOR AND CANADIAN BARRISTER. FOR MY COUNTRY.
Private David Logan, 50th Battalion, April 10th 1917 (age 40)

ENGLAND CALLED, WHO IS FOR LIBERTY? WHO FOR RIGHT? I STOOD FORTH.
Private Sidney Howard Burgess, 10th Battalion, April 9th 1917 (age 26)

Vimy Ridge is remembered as the first battle in which all four Canadian divisions fought together. We would do well to remember, however, that English Canadians of the time tended to think of themselves first and foremost as British North Americans and that the first contingent to go overseas in 1914 could fairly be described as a British army raised in Canada. At Vimy, roughly half the men who went into the attack were born in Canada. Inscriptions on headstones adorned with a maple leaf speak of homes from one end of the country to the other – Au Lac, New Brunswick, Parkhill, Ontario, Roblin, Manitoba, New Westminster, British Columbia – but just as many refer to homes in Britain, from Oban and Stirling in Scotland to Bath and Middlesborough in England. Private George McLauchlan of the 7th Battalion was "a son of the Perthshire mountains," while Captain Claude Harris of the same unit was "the son of Chief Constable Harris, Wakefield, Yorkshire." No matter their birthplace or primary allegiance, they were all British subjects. Vimy certainly infused the feelings of national identity and pride that grew out of the war and loosened the apron strings of the mother country, yet the many professions of loyalty among the epitaphs indicate that in the minds of the soldiers representing the senior Dominion, as of their next of kin, to fight for Canada was to fight for Britain and the ideals of the British Empire.

VOR KARE SON FØDT I THORUP TRANEBJERG, DANMARK. ELSKNET SAVNET.
[OUR DEAR SON, BORN IN THORUP TRANEBJERG, DENMARK. LOVED AND MISSED.]
Private Johan Clemmensen, 87th Battalion, April 14th 1917 (age 19)

VELSIGNET ER DIT MINDE.
[HONOURED BE THY MEMORY.]
Lance Corporal Svend Owen Rose, 24th Battalion, April 9th 1917 (age 20)

HIER RUST ONZE DIERBARE ZOON. GEB. ROTTERDAM.
[HERE RESTS OUR BELOVED SON. BORN IN ROTTERDAM.]
Private Petrus Hendrikus van der Heyden, 1st Canadian Mounted Rifles, April 12th 1917 (age 29)

ZA OTATSBINU I SAVEZNIKA ŽIVOT SVOJ DAO.
[FOR HIS FATHERLAND AND ALLY HE GAVE HIS LIFE.]
Private Chris Meti, Princess Patricia's Canadian Light Infantry, April 10th 1917 (age 22)

A SON OF THE UNITED STATES WHO VOLUNTEERED FOR CANADA.
Private Albert Rhiner, 24th Battalion, April 17th 1917 (age 38)

The question of motives and allegiance takes on other aspects. Rarely, if ever mentioned in accounts of the battle, are the men of different nationalities present at Vimy Ridge. Danish and Dutch volunteers, coming from small, neutral countries bordering Germany, who saw an Allied victory as the surest way to preserve their equally vulnerable homelands from Belgium's fate; a young Serbian immigrant who enlisted in Toronto on his twentieth birthday to fight both for his adoptive country and for the very survival of his native land; and the many Americans who headed "over there" in Canadian khaki long before their own country entered the war. And there are isolated tributes to the fallen from the other Canada, the one that did not rally to Britain's side – the young French Canadians, strangers by language and denomination to their English Canadian countrymen, anomalies in the British Empire's order of battle, misguided participants in an English war in the opinion of their compatriots, who nevertheless strove to uphold the honour and reputation of their people on the field of battle. The 22nd (French Canadian) Battalion that made its name at Courcelette did its part at Vimy Ridge, and the *bons canayens* who lie there still deserve the recognition and respect that has so belatedly come to them.

MORT À VIMY À L'AGE DE 30 ANS EN COMBATTANT POUR LA GRANDE CAUSE.
[DIED AT VIMY AT THE AGE OF 30 FIGHTING FOR THE GREAT CAUSE.]
Private Arthur Goyette, 22nd (French Canadian) Battalion, April 11th 1917

J'AI FAIT MON DEVOIR.
[I DID MY DUTY.]
Private Francis Laflamme, 4th Canadian Mounted Rifles, April 11th 1917 (age 30)

Opposite: A map of Vimy Ridge such as the Topographical Section would have prepared. It shows the contours and features that the planners had to take into account in coordinating a four-division assault supported by a carefully timed series of artillery barrages.

The paucity of inscriptions in French raises the spectre of a deeply embittering controversy just as much a part of the legacy of Vimy Ridge as the deeds of the soldiers. The glorification of Vimy could not, and did not, unite all Canadians behind a stirring national epic of shared sacrifice and triumph. For French Canadians, as for others of non-British stock, the defining episode of the war was the imposition of conscription, which did more to alienate French from English Canadians than any other issue. It is the forgotten irony of Vimy Ridge that the casualties forced the government's hand on the dreaded question of compulsory military service. The battle coincided with the stark moment of truth in Ottawa that the once mighty stream of voluntary recruitment had dried up, and that if the Canadian Corps were to be kept at full strength for a war with no end in sight, conscription, whatever the political cost, was the only resort. Once anathema to Britain and her Dominions, till then proudly distinguished from both allies and enemies by the tradition of voluntary military service, conscription was introduced four months after Vimy and confirmed by the most blatantly manipulated election in Canadian history.

ENLISTED VOLUNTARILY.
Corporal Aimé Lefebvre, 4th Canadian Mounted Rifles, April 10th 1917 (age 19)

WHEN HIS COUNTRY CALLED HE CAME.
Sergeant George Hugh Walter, 24th Battalion, April 9th 1917 (age 33)

EQUALLY READY AT THE CALL OF COUNTRY AND AT THE CALL OF GOD.
Private James Campbell Currie, 102nd Battalion, April 9th 1917 (age 27)

The many Canadian epitaphs proudly proclaiming the soldier's voluntary enlistment acquire a different tone in the wake of the conscription crisis. The polarizing effect on French–English relations remains all too well known, but conscription also pitted anti-conscriptionist farmers, industrial workers, and Canadians of non-British ancestry against its most ardent supporters, the soldiers themselves and the families with members overseas. It is difficult not to suspect that more than one such inscription on Vimy and later graves was composed with a sidelong glance at the neighbour down the road whose husband had avoided his patriotic and Christian duty until compelled, or the farmer in the next concession over whose hale and hearty sons had been granted exemptions for agricultural labour.

The recriminations Canadians hurled at one another over conscription were symptomatic of the terrible strain of the war, bearable only in the belief that grim perseverance would bring the struggle to its one acceptable conclusion. At a time when the war effort was exacerbating the country's internal conflicts and inducing tremors along its greatest fault line, Vimy Ridge demonstrated that the soldiers were doing their part in a cause that most Canadians believed to be necessary and just.

Opposite: One of the two reclining figures, female and male, representing the mothers and fathers in mourning; they flank the steps leading up to the Vimy Memorial.

OBJECTIVE GAINED.
Major Edward Cecil Horatio Moore, 38th Battalion, April 9th 1917 (age 40)

A NATION SPOKE TO A NATION.
Lieutenant John Lant Youngs MC, 1st Battalion, April 9th 1917 (age 21)
[Rudyard Kipling, *Our Lady of the Snows*]

A GLORIOUS DEATH IS A LIVING MEMORY.
Private William Ernest Hill, 116th Battalion, April 9th 1917 (age 31)

THANKS BE TO GOD WHO GIVETH US THE VICTORY.
Lieutenant Edwin Austin Abbey, 4th Canadian Mounted Rifles, April 10th 1917 (age 23)

Canada is perhaps the only belligerent of the Great War whose national memory of the conflict is centred on a victory. Though dearly bought, Vimy Ridge was no Verdun. It did not compound a long list of casualties with the despair of failure or futility, and thus held out consolation denied to the Australians and New Zealanders honouring the courage of the Anzacs at Gallipoli, the Newfoundlanders remembering Beaumont-Hamel, or the British haunted by the first day on the Somme. In the context of 1917, Vimy shone forth as a rare Allied triumph when the prospect of victory was dimmed by the French mutinies, the collapse of Russia, the Italian disaster at Caporetto, the insoluble U-boat menace, and the ghastly expenditure of British and Empire lives for so little ground in Flanders. Vimy was also the first in a series of noteworthy Canadian exploits in 1917, including successful actions at Fresnoy and Hill 70 and culminating with the capture of Passchendaele, which lent an aura of invincibility to the Canadian Corps and raised it to elite status among the formations of the British Empire. Notwithstanding the usurious casualty rates, in the bleakest year of the war Canadians could pride themselves on fielding the one national corps that had risen to every challenge put before it.

It would be a mistake on our part today, however, and a disservice to Canadians of a more devout generation to interpret the preeminence of Vimy Ridge in purely military or secular terms. The most potent symbolic meaning they attached to Vimy surpasses our understanding if we fail to take note of the day on which the battle began.

EASTER MORN.
Sergeant Charles Gordon Riley, 24th Battalion, April 9th 1917 (age 21)

Opposite, above, left: The first Vimy memorials were put up by Canadian soldiers shortly after the battle. Above, right: The First Division memorial and the dedicatory inscription. Below, left: The memorial placed by the Canadian Field Artillery and Canadian Garrison Artillery. Below, right: The memorial to the Third Division.

That April 9th was Easter Monday was an unplanned coincidence that nevertheless seemed nothing short of providential to a population yearning for a higher purpose and consolation in its time of greatest trial and loss. Its connection with the holiest day in the Christian calendar made Vimy Ridge a metaphor for the hill of Golgotha and the battle a lesser Calvary in which the soldiers, in willing emulation of the Redeemer, had laid down their lives for others. In a war seen as no less than a struggle for Christian civilization, a contest between good and evil, their sacrifice elevated Vimy from a military to a spiritual triumph that would open the way to a world purged of the sins and iniquities that had brought the conflict about – militarism, aggression, lawlessness, the lust for power. In itself proof of a divinely sanctioned cause, the victory strengthened the consoling vision of redemption through sacrifice that the Canadian churches had offered in response to a catastrophe otherwise inexplicable in theological terms. How receptive the bereaved were to the image of the fallen soldier as a faithful servant of Christ is evident in the number of Scriptural passages, hymns, and prayers they chose as epitaphs. To people reared in the King James Version of the Bible, who knew the stories behind the passages and read their own lives by their light, the promise of reward and resurrection for the legions of dead scarcely out of their boyhood compensated the fallen for the loss of their achingly young lives, kept the bond of love intact, and gave hope to the mourners of an eventual reunion. Had Jesus not reassured the disciples of His love for them the night before He died, had He not in the days before His death restored their brother Lazarus to the sorrowing Mary and Martha, and had He not blessed and received all whose faith had made them whole? Was not this new generation of saviours equally worthy of salvation and life everlasting?

GREATER LOVE HATH NO MAN
THAN HE LAY DOWN HIS LIFE FOR HIS BROTHER.
Sergeant George Fitton MM, 58th Battalion, April 13th 1917 (age 20)
[Cf. John 15:13]

Two of the many carvings left by Canadian soldiers sheltering in a cavern west of the ridge during the weeks leading up to the assault.

CHRIST JESUS DIED FOR OUR SINS. PRAYER CHANGES THINGS.
Private Mahlon Ezra Spies, 15th Battalion, April 9th 1917 (age 24)

WHO DIES FOR HIM SHALL EVER LIVE. LIVING FOR EVER IN OUR LOVE ENSHRINED.
Private Griffith Ernest Dudley, 24th Battalion, April 12th 1917 (age 20)

AND HE, CASTING AWAY HIS GARMENT, ROSE AND CAME TO JESUS.
Lance Corporal Louis Gordon Beckett, 87th Battalion, April 9th 1917 (age 29)
[Mark 10:50]

HE FOLLOWED IN HIS TRAIN.
Lieutenant Alfred Snow Churchill, Royal Canadian Regiment, April 9th 1917 (age 22)
[Hymn, *The Son of Man Goes Forth to War*]

I AM THE RESURRECTION AND THE LIFE. THY BROTHER SHALL RISE AGAIN.
Lance Sergeant Robert Gunn, 7th Battalion, April 8th/10th 1917 (age 43)
[John 11:25; 23]

LET NOT YOUR HEART BE TROUBLED; I GO TO PREPARE A PLACE FOR YOU.
Private Henry Littler, 54th Battalion, April 9th 1917 (age 20)
[John 14:1; 2]

IN HIS LOVE AND IN HIS PITY HE REDEEMED THEM.
Private Herbert Richard Butt, 102nd Battalion, April 9th 1917 (age 22)
[Isaiah 63:9]

IF WE SUFFER, WE SHALL ALSO REIGN WITH HIM.
Sergeant David Ainslie Hunter, 102nd Battalion, April 9th 1917 (age 26)
[II Timothy 2:12]

THOU LORD, THEIR CAPTAIN IN THE WELL-FOUGHT FIGHT. HALLELUJAH
Lieutenant Frederick Gundy Scott, Canadian Field Artillery, April 20th 1917 (age 21)

WHO DIES FOR THEE AND THINE WINS THEE AT LAST. FOR HIS COUNTRY'S SAKE.
Private Harry Samuel Aldous, 75th Battalion, April 9th 1917 (age 22)

MAY HIS NAME IN THY BOOK BE BOUND, LORD, ON THE RESURRECTION DAY.
Lance Corporal William Ethelbert Taylor, 54th Battalion, April 9th 1917 (age 25)

MAY HIS REWARD BE AS GREAT AS HIS SACRIFICE. AT REST. LOVING WIFE & SONS
Private Thomas James Mathers, 15th Battalion, April 9th 1917 (age 26)

"THOU GAVEST HIM LENGTH OF DAYS FOR EVER" PSA. XXI. IV
Private John Duncan Beurley Craig, 54th Battalion, April 9th 1917 (age 18)

WE HAVE A BUILDING OF GOD, AN HOUSE NOT MADE WITH HANDS ETERNAL IN THE HEAVENS.
Private Ernest Percival Lewis, 4th Canadian Mounted Rifles, April 9th 1917 (age 18)
[II Corinthians 5:1]

CHOSEN OF GOD AND PRECIOUS.
Sergeant George Alan Cunningham, 25th Battalion, April 9th 1917 (age 25)
[I Peter 2:4]

STUDENT AND SOLDIER OF CHRIST. SON OF REV. & MRS. C. THOMSON, C.I.M.
Private Andrew Bennett Thomson, 72nd Battalion, April 9th 1917 (age 20)
[China Inland Mission]

QUE TON SACRIFICE ET NOS PRIÈRES T'OUVRENT LES PORTES DU CIEL. LA FAMILLE
[MAY YOUR SACRIFICE AND OUR PRAYERS OPEN THE GATES OF HEAVEN TO YOU. THE FAMILY]
Private Armand Crevier, Royal Canadian Regiment, April 9th 1917 (age 28)

O SOUL OF MY SOUL, I SHALL MEET THEE AGAIN.
Private John Merritt Wheaton, 85th Battalion, April 9th 1917 (age 19)

NO HOME CAN NOW BE HOME TO ME UNTIL AGAIN YOUR FACE I SEE WHEN JESUS COMES. MOTHER
Sergeant John Moore, 102nd Battalion, April 9th 1917 (age 25)

HONOUR THY FATHER AND THY MOTHER. HE DID.
Private Arnold Gordon MacArthur, 42nd Battalion, April 9th 1917 (age 23)

If Canada's 66,000 war dead were enshrined as an elect in the national memory, the 3,598 soldiers killed at Vimy formed an elect within that elect. It is the battle most often named in the epitaphs, conferring a singular distinction not only upon the soldiers who fell there but upon those who fought at Vimy only to meet their death in some less renowned place. Young men from all walks

Opposite: A sign warning visitors not to venture into terrain still dangerous from unexploded shells.

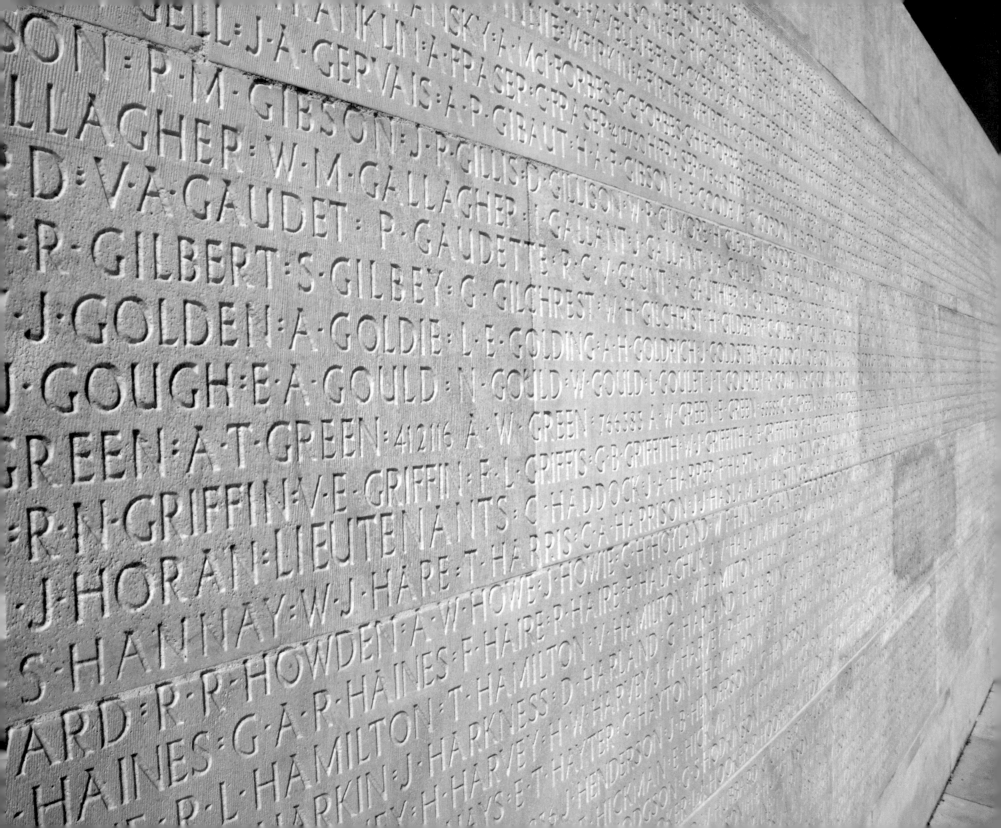

of life save for soldiering, they had confronted the most militaristic of enemies on his terms and prevailed. With the qualities they had shown, magnified by those projected onto them, they had embodied the country at its finest and given an obscure Dominion of the British Empire a foundation of lasting pride and nationhood. Cast in this ennobled, sacrificial image, they had also offered a weary and fractious and grief-stricken population a ray of hope that out of all the toils and suffering of the war a better country and a better world would emerge. To fulfill this hope was the debt the survivors owed to those who had "loved not their lives unto the death" and by their selflessness reminded a flawed humanity of its highest ideals and purpose.

BORN MONTREAL, SEPT. 1 1890. KILLED IN ACTION, VIMY RIDGE.
Sergeant Henry William Nesbitt, Princess Patricia's Canadian Light Infantry, April 9th 1917 (age 26)

IN LOVING MEMORY OF OUR SON WHO MADE THE SUPREME SACRIFICE AT VIMY RIDGE.
Private Thomas Grenville Aldous, 38th Battalion, April 9th 1917 (age 20)

KILLED IN ACTION, VIMY RIDGE.
Private Frank Lewis Portmore, 54th Battalion, April 9th 1917 (age 43)

IN LOVING MEMORY OF FRED EYDEN, KILLED AT VIMY. SADLY MISSED BY WIFE & BOY.
Sergeant Major Frederick Eyden, 16th Battalion, April 9th 1917

BORN IN PERTH, ONT., 3RD OCTOBER 1898. WOUNDED AT VIMY RIDGE. AGED 18 YEARS.
Private Alvin Smith Wilson, 75th Battalion, April 19th 1917

KILLED AT VIMY RIDGE. GONE BUT NOT FORGOTTEN.
Private George Milne, 7th Battalion, April 13th 1917 (age 32)

WOUNDED AT VIMY RIDGE. BORN FORT WILLIAM, CANADA, AUGUST 10, 1897.
Private William Victor Coo, 43rd Battalion, April 15th 1917 (age 19)

WOUNDED AT VIMY RIDGE, FRANCE, APRIL 9TH 1917. A DEARLY BELOVED AND HONOURED SON.
Private John Alexander Cameron, 16th Battalion, October 23rd 1918 (age 23)

GREAT HEARTS ARE GLAD WHEN IT IS TIME TO GIVE.
Lieutenant Colonel Daniel Isaac Vernon Eaton, Royal Canadian Horse Artillery, April 11th 1917 (age 46)

Opposite: The names of 11,245 Canadian soldiers who were killed in France and have no known grave are carved into the walls forming the base of the Vimy Memorial – a list laboriously compiled but not free of error or omission.

'TIS ONLY THOSE THAT HAVE LOVED & LOST CAN REALIZE THE BITTER COST.
WIFE & DAUGHTERS

Sergeant Matthew Tickner, 4th Canadian Mounted Rifles, April 9th 1917 (age 43)

WITH US YOU LIVE. WIFE AND BABIES

Private William Albert Durant, 72nd Battalion, April 12th 1917 (age 24)

ALAS! WHAT LINKS OF LOVE THAT MORN HAS WAR'S RUDE HAND ASUNDER TORN.

Private James Winning Chapman, Canadian Machine Gun Corps, April 9th 1917 (age 26)

[Sir Walter Scott, "The Field of Waterloo"]

'TIS HARD TO PLANT IN SPRING AND NEVER REAP THE AUTUMN YIELD.

Private Harry Lilley, 60th Battalion, April 9th 1917 (age 24)

HONORED AND LOVINGLY REMEMBERED BY HIS MOTHER.

Private John Roland Weir, 10th Battalion, April 9th 1917 (age 17)

TO OUR ONLY SON. ONLY GOD KNOWS HOW WE LOVED HIM ALWAYS.
MOTHER, DAD & MAY

Lance Corporal Charles Amos Jordan, 20th Battalion, April 9th 1917 (age 20)

OUR ONE & ONLY.

Sergeant John Francis Mooney, 38th Battalion, April 9th 1917 (age 28)

HE WAS ALWAYS KIND AND GENEROUS.

Private Charles Edward Bowman, 44th Battalion, April 9th 1917 (age 21)

CHILD OF MY LOVE, COME TO THY HOME, NO MORE IN EXILE NEED THEE ROAM.

Private William Herbert White, 78th Battalion, April 11th 1917 (age 37)

A MAN WHO WAS STRAIGHT IN ALL THINGS AND BELOVED AND RESPECTED BY ALL.

Private George Green, 102nd Battalion, April 9th 1917 (age 37)

DEARLY LOVED, DEEPLY LAMENTED. MY GOD, THY WILL BE DONE.

Lance Corporal John Harold Reeves DCM, 20th Battalion, April 9th 1917 (age 37)

The central avenue at Cabaret Rouge British War Cemetery, into which 7,662 of the fallen (including 749 Canadians) were gathered from temporary burial grounds on the Vimy front. Nearly 5,000 are unidentified.

One by one, the epitaphs of the men who fell at Vimy reconstruct an important part of the experience and reactions of people we will never know to an event that has passed from living into historical memory. Although in name inhabitants of the same country, the Canadians of 1917 would be strangers to us today, and the differences between their time and ours will likely be very pronounced during the commemorations of Vimy Ridge. Even the one legacy of Vimy shared across the years, a deep sense of national pride, cannot be as intense and necessary for us as it was for them and does not serve the same urgent purpose in tempering the sorrow of a country in grief. Nor would we as readily accept, or make part of present-day commemorations, the religious significance with which they invested the battle. Inevitably, with the passage of time, the human tragedy has become abstract, whereas they could put faces to the names of the Glorious Dead and recall them as living beings. But for those who consider themselves friends of the past, the centenary of Vimy Ridge is a chance to look at the battle objectively and focus on the human rather than the mythic elements of an undeniable turning point in Canadian history. No doubt on that dramatic Easter morn a century ago, many a man prayed that this cup might pass from him, or wished himself back at home, then as the barrage lifted took a last look at a cherished photograph and went out to face what had to be faced. To all but a very few Canadians today – and we should give thanks for this – the soldier's sensations and memories of the battle lie beyond our ken, no matter the accuracy and detail of the descriptions; but if we cannot relate to that experience, we can surely feel more than distant sympathy for a lonely widow, a mother no more, pining for a son "loved beyond all human thought," or the French-Canadian mother using her son's epitaph to ask the mothers of her ancestral land in their common tongue to take her into their hearts and say a prayer as they passed by a grave that she herself would never see. We can also note with sadness that the dearest hope of that generation, represented in the *Breaking of the Sword* sculpture on the Vimy Memorial, was not to be realized. The fears that another conflict would engulf their children proved all too true when the countries that had drawn a different set of conclusions from the Great War launched another to overturn its results. Among the headstones in the Bretteville-sur-Laize Canadian War Cemetery in Normandy is one inscribed with a tender message of farewell from a young wife to a husband killed in 1944. Her name was Vimy Ridge Piercy.

Opposite: Isaiah 2:4: "And He shall judge among the nations, and shall rebuke many people: and they shall beat their swords into plowshares, and their spears into pruninghooks: nation shall not lift up sword against nation, neither shall they learn war any more." The Breaking of the Sword makes a visual echo of this famous scriptural passage prophesying an end to war and expresses the dearest hope of the generation that passed through the ordeal of the Great War.

2 FAREWELL, BELOVED

We may start with a flight of fancy to introduce the epitaphs as the remarkable and revealing witness to the past that they are. Imagine archaeologists at some distant time in the future coming upon the British memorials and war cemeteries clustered along the old Western Front. Let us suppose, too, that although the written sources for the Great War no longer survive, the mandate of the War Graves Commission to maintain the monuments in perpetuity has ensured a good state of preservation. Just as archaeologists test the historicity of the Trojan War against evidence from Bronze Age sites, or reconstruct the workings of the Roman army from its camps and fortifications, our imagined archaeologists would set about collating and interpreting the details in the commemorative monuments to form a reasonably coherent picture of the Great War. They would infer from the concentration of the war cemeteries that it had been a very static conflict; from the dates, regiments, and nationalities recorded on the headstones they could develop a chronology of events and a latter-day "Catalogue of Ships" listing the peoples drawn from all over the world into the British Empire's order of battle. The number of nameless graves, tallying with the lists inscribed on the memorials to the missing, would induce recognition of a frighteningly destructive war that inflicted not only mass death but mass annihilation. Some explanation for this would emerge from the insignia on the headstones identifying artillerymen, machine gunners, tank crewmen, flyers, and engineers, which bear witness to the advances in military technology that made such an inflexible war so consumptive of human life. Archaeologists attuned to the contradictory logic of human affairs might perceive the trap into which the belligerents worked themselves, that victory alone, at any price, could redeem the losses that mounted with each year of the war. They might also be intrigued by the presence of graves with a later set of dates, suggesting that this titanic conflict had led not to a lasting settlement but to an even worse calamity.

The evidence responding to the basic questions of who fought the war, and when and where and how it was fought, would lead to further inquiry. Anyone beholding the monuments and war cemeteries would marvel at the effort involved in creating them and at the scrupulous desire to commemorate every last one of the fallen by name, signs of the debt that the survivors felt they owed to the dead. In seeking answers to the very human and very taxing questions as to how people at the time justified so costly a struggle, and how the victors rationalized the appalling price of victory, our future archaeologists would seize upon the thousands of inscriptions engraved at the base of the headstones. As they assembled a corpus of epitaphs and began to categorize the texts by form, content, and theme, they might well see these examples as illustrative of the spirit and purpose behind the creation of the war cemeteries.

AFTER THE WAR WHEN THE DAY WAS O'ER, LAID AWAY ON THE HILLSIDE. GOD BE WITH HIM.
Private William Marks, 15th Battalion, April 26th 1915 (age 18)

BRITANNIA, GUARD WELL IN PEACE OUR LOVED ONE'S RESTING PLACE.
Private George Albert Potts, 5th Battalion, November 25th 1917 (age 39)

OUR DEAD ARE NEVER DEAD TO US UNTIL WE HAVE FORGOTTEN THEM.
Private John Cameron Robertson, 14th Battalion, March 6th 1916 (age 29)

'TIS THE MARK OF A NATION'S HERO, THE SIGN OF A MOTHER'S LOSS.
Private James Rolandson Hewitt, 43rd Battalion, March 6th 1918 (age 33)

IN MEMORY EVER DEAR. EVERY NOBLE DEED LASTS LIKE A GRANITE MONUMENT.
Private William David Wellard, 44th Battalion, May 6th 1917 (age 23)

WE ARE BROTHERS & COMRADES. WE LIE SIDE BY SIDE AND OUR FAITH & OUR HOPES ARE THE SAME.
Private William John Ellins, 3rd Battalion, June 24th 1916 (age 40)

HE SLEEPS BESIDE HIS COMRADES IN A SOLDIER'S GRAVE IN A FOREIGN LAND.
Sapper Rymer Chapman, Canadian Railway Troops, September 4th 1917 (age 21)

FROM A HOMESTEAD, QUANTOCK, SASK. HIS SERVANTS SHALL SERVE HIM.
Private Ayrton Wragge, 13th Battalion, September 6th 1916
[Revelation 22:3]

SON OF JAMES LOUDON LL.D. PRESIDENT, UNIVERSITY OF TORONTO.
Lieutenant Loudon Brian Melville Loudon, 15th Battalion, September 1st 1918 (age 25)

DEARLY BELOVED SON OF MAJ. GEN. S.C. MEWBURN C.M.G.
MINISTER OF MILITIA & DEFENCE, CANADA, AND MARY MEWBURN.
Lieutenant John Chilton Mewburn, 18th Battalion, September 15th 1916 (age 22)

FILS DE G.F.B. ET D'A. LAFRANÇOIS, VERCHÈRES, P.Q., CANADA. LATE DEPUTY MINISTER OF CANADA.
Private Pierre Baillairge, 22nd (French Canadian) Battalion, May 4th 1918 (age 20)

Opposite: Rows of headstones at Étaples Military Cemetery, site of a large base hospital on the French coast south of Boulogne, where 1,148 Canadians are found among the nearly 11,000 burials.

I OWE ALL TO MY ANGEL MOTHER.
Private David Angus Morrison, 46th Battalion, May 8th 1915 (age 27)

LONGING TO SEE HIM, TO HEAR HIM SAY MOTHER.
Private Stanley Aylett, 16th Battalion, September 4th 1916 (age 28)

MOTHER'S DARLING.
Private William Edward Dailey, 4th Battalion, September 7th 1916 (age 16)

GIVE A GENTLE THOUGHT, A SILENT TEAR, A MOTHER'S ONLY LOVE LIES HERE.
Private Francis Sydney Coldwell, 13th Battalion, November 24th 1917 (age 19)

TELL MY MOTHER I WILL MEET HER AT THE FOUNTAIN.
Private William Garfield Rankin, Royal Canadian Regiment, April 22nd 1916 (age 17)

CAN'T FORGET THAT PARTING KISS THAT SEALED YOUR LOVE FOR ME. MOTHER
Private Edward Phillips, 58th Battalion, October 2nd 1918 (age 23)

THE SHELL THAT STILLED HIS TRUE BRAVE HEART BROKE MINE. MOTHER
Corporal James Edward Noble, 25th Battalion, June 13th 1918 (age 21)

SON OF MY HEART, LIVE FOR EVER. THERE IS NO DEATH FOR YOU AND ME.
Private Hal Sutton, 5th Battalion, May 22nd 1915 (age 18)

FORGIVE, O LORD, A MOTHER'S WISH THAT DEATH HAD SPARED HER SON.
Sergeant Thomas Armstrong, 28th Battalion, January 31st 1916 (age 25)

EVER ABSENT, EVER NEAR, STILL I SEE THEE, STILL I HEAR, YET I CANNOT REACH YOU, DEAR MOTHER
Private Percy Sprunt, 8th Battalion, June 14th 1916 (age 23)

LOVED AND ONLY CHILD. SO REST MAY HE, HIS FAULTS LIE GENTLY ON HIM. MOTHER
Private Gordon Moffat, 102nd Battalion, October 1st 1918 (age 25)

Opposite: Inspired by the Mater Dolorosa (Sorrowing Mother) of Christian iconography, the figure of Canada Bereft symbolizes the country's grief for her fallen, represented in turn by the sarcophagus at the base of the Vimy Memorial.

Any discussion of the personal inscriptions must first balance their worth against their limitations as sources. Though they echo the sentiments of their time, they speak directly for only a small proportion of the dead and those who commemorated them, as some rough calculations will show. Of the 66,000 Canadians killed in the Great War, nearly 18,000 have no known grave; of the identified graves, just under half carry a personal inscription, many of which repeat formulae ("Rest in peace," "Gone but not forgotten," "Son of ... born in ...") of little more than fleeting interest. The number of inscriptions that offer insight into the minds of the bereaved, individually and collectively, comes to about 3,000 by my count, speaking for about five percent of Canada's war dead. Their form and realm of expression, though not without considerable variety, adhere to the restrictions imposed by the War Graves Commission and by the conventions of the time. Here the exceptions prove useful in illustrating the rules and, more importantly, the latitude shown in their application. When scanning the collection, for instance, it becomes clear that while most inscriptions stay within the prescribed length of 66 characters (including the spaces between words), a great many do not, the most egregious Canadian example being the following, found in the military plot in Bailleul Communal Cemetery Extension:

IN LOVING MEMORY OF LIEUTENANT ALFRED JAMES LAWRENCE EVANS. B.SC.
MCGILL. 1ST CANADIAN DIVISION 7TH DECEMBER 1915. AGED 26 YEARS.
BORN AT QUEBEC. DIED OF WOUNDS RECEIVED ON 23RD NOVEMBER 1915 WHILE IN
COMMAND OF 1ST BDE MINING SEC. 3RD BTN. FRONT LINE TRENCHES, BELGIUM.
MENTIONED IN DESPATCHES FOR GALLANT AND DISTINGUISHED CONDUCT IN
THE FIELD. "THE BRAVE DIE NEVER, BEING DEATHLESS THEY BUT CHANGE THEIR
COUNTRY'S ARMS FOR MORE, THEIR COUNTRY'S HEART."
Lieutenant Alfred James Lawrence Evans, 3rd Battalion, December 7th 1915 (age 26)

Inscriptions of similar length are found on Canadian markers in Britain. Privately dedicated by the soldier's parents or comrades, they were not subjected to the Commission's regulations since they stood in public burial grounds or in churchyards, where they did not detract from the uniformity of the war cemeteries.

Bedford House Cemetery, just south of Ypres (Ieper), artfully integrates the moat and stands of trees once part of the grounds of a chateau. Its enclosures house over 5,000 British and Dominion dead, including 348 Canadians.

"THY WILL BE DONE." ST. MATT. 26: 42
Corporal Harry Jordon Guest, 19th Battalion, September 11th 1916 (age 22)

O DAD MADDEU IDDYNT CANYS NI WYDDANT PA BETH Y MAENT YN EI WNEUTHUR.
[FORGIVE THEM, FATHER, FOR THEY KNOW NOT WHAT THEY DO.]
Private William Evans, 50th Battalion, June 3rd 1917 (age 26)
[Luke 23:34]

TO-DAY THOU SHALT BE WITH ME IN PARADISE.
Private Samuel Frederick James, 14th Battalion, September 2nd 1918 (age 39)
[Luke 23:43]

O MOTHER OF SORROW, FOR THE LOVE OF THIS SON.
Private Charles Labrador, 25th Battalion, July 27th 1916 (age 20)

NOT HERE – RISEN.
Lieutenant Charles Henry Brown, 27th Battalion, November 10th 1917 (age 31)
[cf. Matthew 28:6]

A great many epitaphs consist of borrowed words. For a last farewell on an honoured grave many thought it best to rely on trusted sources, and it seems to have been the assumption on the part of the Commission that next of kin contributing epitaphs would draw from venerable authorities. Those who sought literary passages turned to the authors whose works they had learned in their schooldays, when memory work and recitation were staples of pedagogy. A trawl through school syllabi from the years before the war shows that the poems most often quarried for epitaphs – Tennyson's "Ode on the Death of the Duke of Wellington" ("The path of duty was the way to glory"), "Break, break, break" ("O for the touch of a vanished hand and the sound of a voice that is still") or Shelley's "Adonais" ("He hath outsoared the shadow of our night") – were required reading for high-school matriculants in English, who, like all students of the time, went through a thoroughly Anglocentric curriculum. Sunday school, following or followed by church, immersed people from an early age in the hymns and writings, particularly John Bunyan's *The Pilgrim's Progress* and John Henry Newman's "Lead, Kindly Light," which provided a plentiful source of spiritual comfort. But if the generation raised before the war entrusted the expression of its grief, acceptance, or hope to one book, it was to the King James Version of the Bible.

Opposite: Some of the 10,700 graves in Lijssenthoek War Cemetery; the 1,056 Canadian graves among them represent nearly every Canadian unit that passed through the Ypres Salient during the war.

My favourite reading, 1st bk. Cor. ch. 13.
Private Alfred Ernest Blackmore, 46th Battalion, September 4th 1916

(Assurance) What time I am afraid I will trust in Thee. Ps. 56.3.
Private William Angus Barnes, 19th Battalion, September 13th 1916 (age 25)

O Lord of hosts, blessed is the man that trusteth in Thee. Ps. 84.12.
Private James MacDonald, 1st Canadian Mounted Rifles, May 16th 1916 (age 29)

God hath delivered my soul from the place of hell for He shall receive me. Ps. 49. 15
Driver Charles Percival Maxted, Canadian Engineers, August 3rd 1916 (age 24)

The use of Scripture in the personal inscriptions is a subject in itself. To paraphrase one scholar, knowledge of the King James Version is a prerequisite for entering into the thought-world of the generation that went through the Great War. The above are some of the epitaphs that display the family's awareness of the passages that the soldier read each day and to which he turned in times of trial. The annotated Bible of a Canadian soldier killed in 1918 contains a list of eighteen passages, all from the New Testament, connecting the teachings, experiences, and tribulations of Christ and His followers to the stages of a devoutly Christian soldier's life on active service and, in two texts frequently used as epitaphs – 2 Timothy 4:5–8 ("I have fought the good fight, I have finished the race, I have kept the faith") and Revelation 21: 4 ("And God shall wipe away all tears from their eyes") – to the eventuality of his death and reward. If these readings served as a spiritual anchor for the men in the trenches, other standard selections supplied comfort to the bereaved. The very Victorian habit of reading one's experiences through the lens of the Bible, and charting a path through this earthly pilgrimage by identifying oneself with its stories or characters, guided the next of kin, who in like fashion turned to familiar consolatory passages ("Blessed are they who mourn") or looked to the reassurance of God's covenant with His servants.

Him that cometh to me I will in no wise cast out.
Private Henry Gordon Marchant, Princess Patricia's Canadian Light Infantry, October 31st 1917 (age 28)
[John 6:37]

With long life will I satisfy him. Ps. 91.16.
Private Richard Shea, 27th Battalion, October 2nd 1918 (age 29)

Next of kin seeking to cast their loss in a certain light could do so by selecting passages to make their point indirectly. Quotation from Scripture or literature thus broadened rather than narrowed the range of expression. There are examples to suggest that families cited chapter and verse to give voice to feelings which, phrased in less authoritative tones, might have been rejected as too contentious or hostile. The Psalms, with their pleas for justice and cries for the chastisement of the wicked, provided a rich fund of material for those resorting to implication instead of risking bald statement, as in the first passage below, put in the mouth of a Newfoundland soldier who died as a prisoner of war and was buried in the land of his captors. Similarly oblique references to tyrants, to the Almighty's endorsement of the Allied cause, and the triumph of good over evil condemned the Kaiser and all his works without referring explicitly to the enemy, a practice the Commission discouraged.

I HAVE DONE JUSTICE AND JUDGEMENT. LEAVE ME NOT TO MY OPPRESSORS.
Private Lewis Hudson, Royal Newfoundland Regiment, April 2nd 1918 (age 22)
[Psalm 119:121]

BY THIS I KNOW THOU FAVOUREST ME, THAT MINE ENEMY DOTH NOT TRIUMPH AGAINST ME.
Private Vernon Earle, 27th Battalion, July 11th 1916 (age 31)
[Psalm 41:11]

SCATTER THOU THE PEOPLE THAT DELIGHT IN WAR.
Private Reginald George Aldridge, 5th Battalion, March 16th 1918 (age 25)
[Psalm 68:30]

YOUNG MEN, YE HAVE OVERCOME THE WICKED ONE. I JOHN 2. 13
Private William Gilbert Raymond McGreer, 47th Battalion, August 11th 1918 (age 21)

FOR KING AND COUNTRY THUS HE FELL, A TYRANT'S ARROGANCE TO QUELL.
Private Harrison Raymond Allen, 16th Battalion, December 2nd 1916 (age 25)

"CURST GREED OF GOLD, WHAT CRIMES THY TYRANT POWER HAS CAUSED." VIRGIL
Private Victor Lionel Summers, 28th Battalion, August 9th 1918 (age 31)

Infrequent instances of veiled enmity aside, Scripture and literature served to hallow the sacrifice and memory of the fallen. The depths of love between a wife and husband might also find their most intense expression through Scripture, particularly in the oft-chosen Song of Songs ("Mine till the day break and the shadows flee away"; "Many waters cannot quench love"), or in this richly

allusive passage on the headstone of Private Kenneth MacDonald of the 13th Battalion, killed in March of 1915: "My beloved is unto me as a cluster of camphire in the vineyards of En-Gedi." The great number of personal inscriptions citing the Song of Songs should also remind the present generation, no longer on instantly familiar terms with the King James Version, not to overlook the significance of epitaphs that can sometimes pall through repetition. Though often interpreted in allegorical or mystical ways, the Song of Songs was for the people who lived at the time of the Great War the most powerful pledge of love, especially married love, and the firmest pledge that this love was stronger than death.

THE BLOOD OF CHRIST, GOD'S SON, CLEANSETH US FROM ALL SIN.
Private Ernest Spark McClelland, 1st Battalion, April 15th 1916 (age 23)

JESUS DIED FOR ME. I'M NOT AFRAID TO DIE FOR HIM.
Private Alexander McDonald, Canadian Machine Gun Corps, September 9th 1918 (age 21)

HE DIED FOR OTHERS. EVEN SO DID CHRIST.
Lieutenant Thomas Hart MacKinlay, 29th Battalion, October 26th 1916 (age 28)

HIS LIFE, ONE THOUGHT FOR OTHERS. HIS DEATH, SUFFERING IN SACRIFICE.
Private Frank Asher Povey, Lord Strathcona's Horse, July 10th 1917 (age 21)

WE GRUDGE NOT OUR LIFE IF IT GIVE LARGER LIFE TO THEM THAT LIVE.
Captain Alexander MacGregor, 28th Battalion, August 9th 1918 (age 31)

SACRIFICED THAT WE HOPE WAS FOR DEMOCRACY. MAY HIS SOUL REST IN PEACE.
Private Patrick Thomas Belanger, 21st Battalion, August 6th 1918 (age 24)

LIBERTY AND FREEDOM HAD TO BE WON BY THE WILLING SACRIFICE OF LIFE.
Private William Stanley Mills, 5th Canadian Mounted Rifles, March 26th 1916 (age 23)

DIED FOR KING AND CONSTITUTION WITH WORLD WIDE LIBERTY. GOD IS LOVE.
Lieutenant William Joseph Sanderson Connor, Canadian Field Artillery, July 5th 1916 (age 31)

I COULDN'T DIE IN A BETTER CAUSE (FROM HIS OWN LIPS).
Lance Corporal Clayton Robertson Selkirk, 5th Canadian Mounted Rifles, June 23rd 1917 (age 21)

Opposite: A handful of Canadian, Australian, and New Zealand headstones appear among the 1,507 graves at Coxyde Military Cemetery, north of Ypres, near the Belgian coast.

HE ASKED LIFE OF THEE AND THOU GAVEST HIM A LONG LIFE, EVEN FOR EVER AND EVER.
Private Harold Percy Bridge, 1st Battalion, March 4th 1915 (age 27)
[Psalm 21:4]

"It is finished" – Christ's dying words in the Gospel of John – proclaims the inscription on the headstone of Driver Alex Henderson of the Canadian Field Artillery, who died four days after the Armistice. The war was over, the long agony had ended, and death had been swallowed up in victory. Confronted by a death toll so terrible and benumbing, those burdened with grief were understandably inclined to embrace the idealism or religious faith that made the sacrifice meaningful and necessary. These were not the only barriers against the unwelcome – and unbearable – feeling of despair or futility at so great a loss of life.

I WILL GIVE HIM A WHITE STONE AND IN THE STONE A NEW NAME – VICTORY.
Private Hal Russell Bowers, 47th Battalion, May 5th 1917 (age 23)
[cf. Revelation 2:17]

FOR GOD AND RIGHT. LET NOT A WHISPER FALL THAT OUR HERO DIED IN VAIN.
Lieutenant Lloyd James Daniel Scott, 38th Battalion, September 29th 1918 (age 22)

I LIE HERE, MOTHER, BUT VICTORY IS OURS.
Private Thomas Mack, 8th Battalion, April 29th 1917 (age 24)

Canadians could also take considerable pride in the exploits of their soldiers which, as we have seen with the exaltation of Vimy Ridge, offset the grief of the mourners. The impulse that led people to name schools, streets, geographical features, and even their children after famous victories is evident in the epitaphs uniting the soldier's memory with the battles making up the mosaic of the final victory. A *cursus honorum* of three battles completes the inscription on the headstone of a veteran buried in Toronto, technically not a war death but in his shortened existence just as much a casualty of the Great War as his comrades at rest in France and Flanders. Families no less proudly saluted the soldier's courage in the performance of his duties or the esteem in which his comrades had held him. It is clear from the examples below that they are taken verbatim from letters of condolence that appear to have had the desired effect.

Opposite: Replicas of the signs provided by the Imperial (now Commonwealth) War Graves Commission to guide next of kin to cemeteries south of Ypres (Ieper). They are found in the passageway through the Lille Gate (or Rijsselpoort) beneath the ramparts on the town's southern side.

DEO OPTIMO MAXIMO.
[TO GOD, BEST AND GREATEST.]
Lieutenant Harold Eustace Piercy, 13th Battalion, October 14th 1916 (age 25)

FIDUS ACHATES. BUT HIGH AS HEAVEN THE FAME IS THAT IF WE DIE WE SHARE.
Captain John King Swanson, 46th Battalion, April 13th 1917 (age 27)
[The hero's faithful companion in the *Aeneid*; Algernon Charles Swinburne, "Jacobite Song"]

"HE RUSHED INTO THE FIELD AND FOREMOST FIGHTING FELL." BYRON
Lieutenant John Llewellyn Evans, 54th Battalion, March 1st 1917 (age 23)

OUR WORK MUST BE BROUGHT TO A SATISFACTORY CONCLUSION OR WE DIE IN THE ATTEMPT.
Lieutenant David Grant Davidson, 23rd Battalion, August 23rd 1917 (age 21)

From our later perspective, the epitaphs of the Great War, teeming with historical and human interest, do much to illustrate the attitudes and reactions of Canadians in the years after the Armistice. But they go further than that. They tell us, more convincingly than any other source, why governments and populations in the 1930s were so desperate to cling to peace at almost any price. The appeasement policy and the dishonourable compromises made in hopes of forestalling a second major war are roundly scorned today, especially with the wisdom of hindsight. But appeasement takes on a different hue in the light of the following epitaphs which need no elaboration. What politician could hope to persuade people still reeling from the Great War that they must confront the odious regimes brandishing the threat of a war, even though it promised to be even worse than the one before; and what population would not have urged its leaders to pursue every option or make any concession to avoid the terrible fate visited on these shattered families?

BROTHER CLASP THE HAND OF BROTHER STEPPING FEARLESSLY THROUGH THE NIGHT.
Private Thomas Henry Price, 13th Battalion, September 27th 1916 (age 25)

SIX BROTHERS IN ALL ANSWERED THE CALL. ONE CRIPPLED, THREE KILLED.
Private Robert Scott Chalmers, 5th Battalion, September 1st 1918 (age 37)

ONE SON OF FOUR SERVING HERE. ONE IN ENGLAND. BOTH DIED OF WOUNDS.
Lieutenant Vincent Robert Alexander Crombie MC, 19th Battalion, October 26th 1918 (age 21)

Opposite: A German bunker sits in the still rumpled ground near Zonnebeke; such bunkers were the key points in the German defences around Passchendaele.

fallen Victoria Cross winner's name by passing it on to his own son, whose epitaph in turn records his fidelity to the memory of his uncle and forebear. The soldier and memoirist Will Bird named his son after a brother killed early in 1915. Less than thirty years later he faced the sad task of composing an epitaph with overtones of loss in two wars.

BORN PORT ALBERT, ONTARIO. SERVED 1914-1918, 1940-1944. "FOUGHT A GOOD FIGHT"
Private Alexander MacKenzie, Canadian Scottish Regiment, June 9th 1944 (age 52)

HE WAS A GOOD SOLDIER AND SERVED HIS COUNTRY IN TWO WARS.
Corporal Clarence Spalding, Corps of Royal Canadian Engineers, June 26th 1944 (age 48)

HIS BROTHERS, JOSEPH EDGAR AND CHARLES RUDOLPH,
WERE KILLED IN FRANCE 16.7.16 AND 27.8.18.
Reverend George Alexander Harris, Canadian Parachute Battalion, June 7th 1944 (age 34)

HE DID HIS DUTY – 1918 & 1942.
REMEMBERED BY LOVING WIFE VALERIE, PETER & GILLIAN.
Sergeant Major Alexander Howden Tough, Calgary Regiment, August 19th 1942 (age 42)

HE FOLLOWED THE TRADITION OF HIS FAMILY AND NAMESAKE,
FRED FISHER, V.C. 1914-1918.
Lieutenant Fred Fisher, Canadian Grenadier Guards, August 8th 1944 (age 23)

HE LIVED, FELT DAWN, SAW SUNSET GLOW, LOVED
AND WAS LOVED – HIS MEMORY REMAINS.
Captain Stephen Stanley Bird, North Nova Scotia Highlanders, July 8th 1944 (age 24)

Opposite: Sunset and long shadows at Bedford House Cemetery.

3

THE YPRES SALIENT

The men of the 1st Canadian Division guarding the rim of the Ypres Salient in the early spring of 1915 had been soldiers for little more than six months. A handful of Boer War veterans and a dash of experienced officers leavened the mix, but aside from summer soldiering in the militia, stints of training at Valcartier and the Salisbury Plain, and a spectator's seat during the British attack at Neuve Chapelle, these citizen volunteers entered the lists as utter neophytes compared with the conscripts and reservists across the way. All German males spent the first two years of their adulthood in compulsory military training and a further five years refreshing their skills in annual manoeuvres with their regiments. Against an army long groomed for war in a technically advanced, thoroughly militarized society, there was a naive confidence that the intrinsic prowess of the Canadian volunteer would prevail. Hardy Canadian militiamen had seen off the Americans in 1812, repulsed the Fenians in 1866, put down the Northwest Rebellion in 1885, and won plaudits in South Africa at the turn of the new century, thus furnishing all the proof needed that Canadians were born soldiers who required only rudimentary training to hold their own with professionals. The most ardent apostles of this militia myth, the Minister of Militia and Defence Sam Hughes first among them, had no wish to be confused either by awkward facts contradicting an article of faith or by the reality that the raw material of the First Contingent was now pitted against an enemy, the likes of which no Canadian soldier had ever encountered, in a war that was about to surpass all previous imaginings.

READY, AYE, READY.
Lance Corporal Peter Johnstone, 16th Battalion, April 22nd 1915 (age 30)

HE GAVE HIS PURE SOUL UNTO HIS CAPTAIN CHRIST.
Lieutenant Guy Melfort Drummond, 13th Battalion, April 22nd 1915 (age 27)

MENTIONED IN DESPATCHES FOR GALLANT AND DISTINGUISHED CONDUCT.
Major Edward Cuthbert Norsworthy, 13th Battalion, April 22nd 1915 (age 35)

IN MEMORY. DIED FIGHTING FOR LIBERTY. EX LONG DISTANCE CHAMPION RUNNER OF SCOTLAND.
Private James Duffy, 16th Battalion, April 23rd 1915 (age 25)

Cyril Barraud *First Glimpse of Ypres*
[CWM 19710261-0021 Beaverbrook Collection of War Art, Canadian War Museum]

DUTY NOBLY DONE FOR KING AND MOTHERLAND.
Private Joseph Crook Bolton, 14th Battalion, April 23rd 1915 (age 32)

PRO PATRIA.
Gunner Vyvyan Ivor Lovekyn, Canadian Field Artillery, April 23rd 1915 (age 20)

VIA SACRA. OF SUCH ARE EMPIRES MADE.
Private Carlton Flatt Burnes, 2nd Battalion, April 24th 1915 (age 23)

REMEMBER, HE WHO YIELDS HIS LIFE, HE'S A SOLDIER AND A MAN.
Private Arthur Ernest Williams, 8th Battalion, April 25th 1915 (age 16)

HE FREELY SERVED.
Private William Penstone Nunn, 3rd Battalion, April 27th 1915 (age 19)

In the first collision with the war's realities, the performance of the Canadian newcomers would demonstrate the truth and the illusion of the militia myth. Twice beclouded with poison gas, repeatedly blasted from their shallow trenches, and fighting a dozen small battles that the senior commanders could not manage as a coherent whole, the isolated Canadian battalions put up resistance that in places simply beggars description. But it was too much to trust solely to the spontaneous heroism of a Major Edward Norsworthy, a Lance Corporal Fred Fisher VC, or a Lieutenant Edward Bellew VC, or to the courageous reactions of so many more who rescued a potentially catastrophic situation. The Second Battle of Ypres lay bare the flaws in command, communication, reconnaissance, tactical decisions, and weaponry that contributed to the loss of roughly 6,000 men killed, wounded, or captured in four days of fighting. The casualty rate of nearly forty per cent in their first battle was to be matched not even by the Somme or Passchendaele. Although the Canadians deserved the praise bestowed upon them for preventing a German breakthrough, it should not be forgotten that nearly half the Canadians taken prisoner in the Great War went into captivity at Second Ypres.

HE FOUGHT AND DIED A HERO. MISSED BY HIS LOVED ONES.
Private Walter McClay, 15th Battalion, April 27th 1915 (age 24)

IN CHRIST HE RESTS, HIS LABOR O'ER EVEN WHEN HIS LIFE WAS JUST BEGUN. R.I.P.
Private Leslie Brownlow Hill, 16th Battalion, April 27th 1915 (age 25)

IN ETERNAL MEMORY FROM FATHER, TOM, FRED, RACHEL, AMY, HARRY, JACK & MARY.
Private Edwin John McKew, 10th Battalion, April 28th 1915 (age 29)

IN MEMORY OF MY DEAR SON. HE GAVE HIS WORD & DIED FOR HOME & COUNTRY. GONE BUT NOT FORGOTTEN.
Corporal Thomas Lang, 13th Battalion, April 28th 1915 (age 38)

HE GAVE HIS ALL, THE ONE WE LOVED, FOR DUTY, LOVE AND HONOUR. HIS MOTHER.
Gunner Frederick John Murray, Canadian Field Artillery, April 28th 1915 (age 20)

Vimy Ridge and Second Ypres were the two battles deemed worthy of separate commemoration by the Canadian Battlefields Memorials Commission. In its attitude of mourning, Frederick Clemesha's *Brooding Soldier* honours the memory of the Canadians subjected to the first use of chemical weapons in modern warfare. It stands at a crossroads named Vancouver Corner in honour of that city's 7th Battalion, which fought with extraordinary tenacity at this crucial hinge of the Canadian line. It was from this area that in the late afternoon of April 22nd, 1915, a turning point in the war, the Canadians first witnessed a sight so strange and horrifying that no two accounts fully agree on the shape and colour of the gas cloud. Though aimed at the French sector immediately to their left, the poisonous miasma drifted into the Canadian lines, where the soldiers felt the effects they had seen in the choking, suffocating Zouaves fleeing in terror towards Ypres. Despite the shock, the Canadians fought a series of holding actions along their exposed flank and put up such stubborn resistance along their front that the Germans launched a second gas attack a day and a half later. Terrible as it was, gas was no longer a surprise, and by now the Canadians had learned to protect themselves by putting soaked cloth over their mouths and noses; but the intense and accurate German shellfire that preceded the gas attack looms even larger in accounts of the battle for its effect in driving the defenders from their positions and forcing them to pull back over open ground. After four days of withstanding unrelenting pressure, the Canadians were at last withdrawn, leaving the dead and dying in the positions they had held to the last.

The Kitcheners' Wood memorial commemorating the first Canadian attack of the war.

The German cemetery near Langemark. Over 44,000 soldiers are buried or commemorated here.

Only a very few of the the Canadians who fell at Second Ypres were to lie in identified graves. The rest, scatttered in ground held by the enemy and fought over many times, became the soldiers known unto God, the myriads of unidentified dead gathered after the war from the fields where *The Brooding Soldier* keeps vigil.

TO FAITHFUL WARRIORS COMES THEIR REST.
Private Albert Scurr, 2nd Battalion, April 22nd 1915 (age 26)

SAVED BY GRACE. THO' LOCKED UP IN SATAN'S PRISON I FROM HERE GO ON TO HEAVEN.
Private Bert Lavender, 2nd Battalion, April 22nd 1915 (age 20)

AND THEY SHALL SEE HIS FACE AND HIS NAME SHALL BE ON THEIR FOREHEADS.
Private Thomas Essington Barker, 3rd Battalion, April 23rd 1915 (age 21)
[Revelation 22:4]

AND JESUS DREW NEAR AND WENT WITH THEM.
Private John Donald Jamieson, 15th Battalion, April 24th 1915 (age 19)
[Luke 24:15]

THE PATRIOT'S BLOOD'S THE SEED OF FREEDOM'S TREE.
Sapper George Newcastle Grieves, Canadian Engineers, April 26th 1915 (age 30)

HONOUR IS THEIRS WHO FOR THEIR COUNTRY DIED, BUT FOR US THE GLORIOUS EXAMPLE.
Driver William Craigie, Canadian Field Artillery, April 30th 1915 (age 29)

WHOSE FATHER, KENNETH JOHN MORRISON, WAS LOST ON THE LUSITANIA, MAY 7 1915.
Driver Albert Henry Morrison, Canadian Field Artillery, July 5th 1917 (age 22)

A VOLUNTEER FROM THE U.S.A. TO AVENGE THE LUSITANIA MURDER.
Driver Leland Wingate Fernald, Canadian Field Artillery, May 8th 1916 (age 28)

The sanctity of the fallen and the cause for which they had given their lives took root in Canadian minds after Second Ypres. To let the epitaph of Private John Campbell speak for all, he and his comrades had "nobly died with face to the foe, slain

Opposite: Trench map of the area around St. Julien and the scene of the Canadian battle in April 1915.
Note Kitcheners' Wood in the lower left quarter; the Brooding Soldier stands at the crossroads below Keerselare in the upper right.

by a ruthless hand." It was not only the number of dead, portending the grim struggle to come, but the manner of their deaths that hallowed their memory in what was clearly a righteous and necessary war against evil incarnate. Two weeks after the use of poison gas padded the docket of German atrocities, a U-boat torpedoed the *Lusitania* with significant loss of Canadian as well as American life, making good on the German threat to sink Allied and neutral ships without warning. The anger at an inhumane enemy constrained by no moral law never faded during the war and remained vivid for years afterwards; and the reaction to "Hunnish" barbarity was to magnify the virtues of the soldiers who in defence of civilization itself had faced the worst this barbaric foe had to offer and still triumphed over him. Strange as it may seem, however, the polarization of good and evil, and the consoling pride that families took in their fallen champions of Christian civilization, find more forceful and frequent expression in the Canadian epitaphs of the First World War than in those of the Second. To a generation that remembered Louvain or Ypres or the *Llandovery Castle*, the crimes of the Nazi regime were horrifying but not unprecedented. They lacked the shock of the new that had provoked such outrage thirty years before.

OUR ONLY BOY IS SLEEPING IN FLANDERS FIELDS WHERE POPPIES BLOW.
Private Albert Edward Walker, 72nd Battalion, September 27th 1918 (age 18)

SHORT DAYS AGO LIVED, FELT DAWN, SAW SUNSET GLOW, LOVED AND WAS LOVED.
Private Thomas MacWatt, 1st Battalion, August 30th 1918 (age 29)

LOVED & WERE LOVED & NOW YOU LIE IN FLANDERS FIELDS.
Sapper Walter Stawell Boxer, Canadian Engineers, December 12th 1917 (age 33)

TO YOU FROM FAILING HANDS WE THROW THE TORCH.
Gunner Horace Eugene Yeomans, Canadian Field Artillery, April 10th 1916 (age 19)

FOR LIBERTY'S CAUSE HE HELPED CARRY THE TORCH UNTIL HE FELL.
Private Skuli Lindal, 27th Battalion, April 15th 1918 (age 24)

IF YE BREAK FAITH WITH US WHO DIE, WE SHALL NOT SLEEP.
Lance Corporal Norman McCallum Smith, 14th Battalion, November 21st 1916 (age 25)

WE WILL KEEP FAITH WITH HIM WHO SLEEPS IN FLANDERS' FIELDS.
Private Wesley John Bell, 5th Battalion, April 9th 1917 (age 23)

THE TORCH YOUR FAILING HANDS PASSED ON IS OURS TO HOLD AND CARRY ON.
Lieutenant John Lawrence Morgan, Royal Canadian Regiment, May 17th 1944 (age 28)

These concrete bunkers, recently restored as a memorial, occupy the site of the first medical dugouts excavated along the spoilbank of the Yser Canal a little to the north of Ypres (Ieper). It was at or near this spot that John McCrae wrote the most famous poem of the war, "In Flanders Fields," in May of 1915, during the Second Battle of Ypres. He did not survive the war, succumbing to pneumonia in January of 1918; he lies buried in Wimereux Cemetery, near Boulogne.

Aerial views of cemeteries and memorials of the Ypres Salient:
1 – Tyne Cot British Cemetery, the largest Commonwealth cemetery in the world
2 – Buttes New British War Cemetery in Polygon Wood, east of Ypres
3 – Bedford House Cemetery
4 – The Menin Gate, built into the ramparts of Ypres and standing over the road along which tens of thousands of British and Dominion soldiers marched out to the Salient

Second Ypres was a crisis narrowly averted that was transformed into a moral victory by the famous poem it spawned. John McCrae's *In Flanders Fields* has made the poppy a universal symbol of remembrance and regeneration, but for Canadians of the time it had a very different resonance. The charge that the dead lay upon the living in the poem, to redeem their sacrifice by seeing the war through to final victory, put the will to prevail into words that embraced loss, sacrifice, and resolve. It became a rallying cry during the war, and a natural source of epitaphs afterwards. It offered sympathy for the dead, a calming image of their resting place, and in the wake of the Allied victory the consoling assurance that they had not died in vain. Its meaning could change with the times as well, for after the war the living now owed it to the fallen to enshrine their memory and to uphold the ideals for which they had died. The injunction not to break faith with those who lay in Flanders fields would go on to acquire fresh urgency in 1939, when the torch was passed to a generation called upon to take up the quarrel with the foe their fathers had faced, and to uphold the victory they had won at such great cost.

Second Ypres had been a terrible initiation, but Canada's soldiers had enabled the Allies to retain a corner of Belgium that by 1915 had come to symbolize Britain and the Empire's determination. The Ypres Salient, a large semicircle bulging out from the Allied front, was to be the Verdun ("they shall not pass") of the British and Dominion armies for forty-seven of the fifty-two months of the Great War. The salient marked the place where the war of movement ground to a halt in 1914 and stagnated into a virtual siege of Ypres that lasted until the final months of the war, with the opposing armies locked in a stalemate that they had neither wished nor planned for. In a landscape so flat as to make the slightest rise seem a local Everest, the Germans ensconced on the low ridges enclosing Ypres like an amphitheatre had commanding views over the orchestra of the salient below and could bring down observed fire from three directions. Since Ypres was the only Belgian town not in German hands and protected the lifeline back to the Channel ports and England, the British had no choice but to hold firm in a soggy target range, be it at an average cost of five thousand dead a month. It was in this cockpit of the Western Front that each of the four Canadian divisions learned its trade over the eighteen months between the Canadians' arrival in Flanders and their departure for the Somme.

In loving memory of our dear son Bugler William Henry Chambers, 58th Canadians, C.E.F. Born at Toronto, Canada, Nov. 13th 1898. Fell mortally wounded at St. Eloi, April 11th 1916. Died of wounds July 5th 1916 at Granville Hospital, Ramsgate. Aged 17 years 7 months. Dearly loved son of Elizabeth and John W. Chambers, Toronto, Canada. He answered his country's call and nobly did his duty.
Private William Henry Chambers, 58th Battalion, July 5th 1916 (age 17)

IN EVER LOVING MEMORY OF ROSSITER JOHN GEORGE ADAMS. ONLY CHILD OF GEORGE A. & ANNIE ADAMS, MAPLE CREEK, CANADA. DIED OCT. 4TH 1918. ALSO OF HIS COUSIN MACDONALD F. HARPER, THIRD SON OF F.J. & PONTINE HARPER. WOUNDED & MISSING AT YPRES, JUNE 13TH 1916.
Private Rossiter John George Adams, 15th Battalion (Reserve), October 4th 1918 (age 21)

KILLED IN ACTION, SANCTUARY WOOD. BEATI MUNDO CORDE.
[BLESSED ARE THE PURE OF HEART.]
Lieutenant Thomas Brehaut Saunders, 13th Battalion, June 13th 1916 (age 20)

AGE 33. DIED OF WOUNDS RECEIVED AT YPRES.
Private Eusèbe Loiseau, 22nd (French Canadian) Battalion, June 29th 1916

The Canadians took their first leave of the salient in the summer of 1916 with the bitter aftertaste of two battles in their mouths. The memory of the second and greater of the two is preserved by the monument placed on Hill 62; the memory of the first, however, a wasteful, demoralizing, and mishandled fiasco that counts among the rare defeats suffered by the Canadian Corps, remains only in the headstones of the soldiers who died there. In retrospect, the battle of the St. Eloi craters outlines the disaster that Passchendaele might well have become but for the experience and skill of seasoned commanders, officers, and other ranks. If any battle dispelled any lingering illusions of the militia myth, St. Eloi was the one to do so. Ordered to take over a series of mine craters blown in the enemy line by British and Canadian tunnellers and captured by British infantry, the men of the relatively untried 2nd Canadian Division were sent floundering into a sleet-swept, shell-pocked moonscape where no one knew which crater was which, which one was held by friend or foe, or how many there in fact were. Told that they were to occupy seven craters, they instead found more than thirty, and ended up fighting for objectives no one could identify. In these ghastly, confusing conditions, the soldiers proved long on courage, their senior officers short on the professional qualities necessary to impose order and purpose on a battle they were conducting largely in their imaginations. The lack of coordination, reconnaissance, and communication resulted in the painful cession of ground painfully won, and the loss of 1,400 casualties – sad examples, if any were needed, of the lives swallowed up in struggles to capture a bit of the enemy's quagmire.

GOODNIGHT, BELOVED, NEVER GOODBYE. MOTHER
Private Lawrence Hardman, 24th Battalion, April 2nd 1916 (age 20)

Opposite: Map showing the trenchlines and contours southeast of Ypres where the Canadians fought so desperately in June of 1916. Note Maple Copse (between quadrants 23 and 24), now the site of the cemetery shown at the beginning of this chapter.

HIS GIFT.
Private Charles Johnson, 2nd Battalion, April 3rd 1916 (age 27)

AFFECTIONATE ONLY SON.
Private Francis Richard Graham, 58th Battalion, April 4th 1916 (age 19)

YOU WILL NEVER BE FORGOTTEN BY YOUR LOVING MOTHER, DEAR BOY.
Private Ernest Gatehouse, 49th Battalion, April 5th 1916 (age 19)

A SOLDIER AND A MAN.
Sergeant Joseph William Fowlie, 49th Battalion, April 7th 1916 (age 38)

MI AYMDRECHAIS YMDRECH DEG.
[I HAVE FOUGHT THE GOOD FIGHT.]
Private Tom Davies, 49th Battalion, April 12th 1916 (age 32)

A CANADIAN BOY WHO GAVE HIS LIFE FOR THE EMPIRE AND FREEDOM.
Private Thomas Mills, 4th Battalion, April 12th 1916 (age 28)

THE ANGEL OF THE LORD ENCAMPETH ROUND ABOUT THEM THAT FEAR HIM AND DELIVERETH THEM.
Private Peter Slaven, 13th Battalion, April 19th 1916 (age 27)
[Psalm 34:7]

A LOVING BROTHER, A GOOD CHUM, FAITHFUL SOLDIER AND FRIEND. GOODNIGHT
Private William Munro MacDonald, 15th Battalion, April 20th 1916 (age 31)

HE BEING DEAD YET SPEAKETH. UNDERNEATH ARE THE EVERLASTING ARMS.
Sergeant Major Stanley Victor Perry, Canadian Field Artillery, April 20th 1916 (age 29)

THAT WHICH HE KNEW NOT, FATHER – TEACH. PARDON HIS UNTOLD SINS – BESEECH.
Gunner William Henry Pettit, Canadian Field Artillery, April 24th 1916 (age 24)

FIRST CANADIAN CONTINGENT. R.I.P. WE WILL NEVER FORGET.
Private Austin Keens, 15th Battalion, April 28th 1916 (age 24)

Opposite: Railway Dugouts Burial Ground (Transport Farm) is situated in the middle of quadrant 21 of the map on the previous page. Most of its 636 Canadian fallen were killed in the fighting around Hill 62 in June of 1916.

IN THE BEAUTY AND STRENGTH OF EARLY MANHOOD.
Captain Ross Penner Cotton, 16th Battalion, June 13th 1916 (age 23)

IN LOVING MEMORY OF OUR SON. HE DIED IN DEFENCE OF OUR HOME & COUNTRY.
Private Ronald Wilson Riley, 5th Battalion, June 13th 1916

HE CHOSE AS HIS MOTTO, DUTY FIRST, AND HE KEPT IT EVEN UNTO DEATH.
Lance Corporal Charles Marshall Taylor, 13th Battalion, June 13th 1916 (age 25)

REMEMBER HIM WITH HONOUR AND THANKSGIVING.
Driver Bertram John Tucker, Canadian Field Artillery, June 13th 1916 (age 23)

DEAR JIM, SOMEDAY—SOMETIME, WE'LL UNDERSTAND.
LOVING SISTERS AND BROTHERS
Private James MacKenzie, 7th Battalion, June 13th 1916 (age 17)

2ND LIEUT. 7TH U.S. INFANTRY.
A GALLANT SOLDIER UNDER HIS OWN AND HIS ADOPTED FLAG.
Captain Stanley Willis Wood, 16th Battalion, June 13th 1916 (age 29)

THE LORD KNOWETH THEM THAT ARE HIS.
Gunner George Alexander MacDiarmid, Canadian Field Artillery, June 13th 1916 (age 27)

KILLED IN ACTION ON DUTY.
Private Frederick Charles Merriam, 16th Battalion, June 13th 1916 (age 37)

REJECTED FOUR TIMES, ACCEPTED THE FIFTH. REST AFTER LABOUR.
Private Charles Turner, 10th Battalion, June 16th 1916 (age 22)

"I WEAR THE CROSS, HE WEARS THE CROWN." MOTHER AND DAD
Sapper James Charles Murray, Canadian Engineers, June 16th 1916 (age 20)

VIRTUTIS GLORIA MERCES.
[GLORY IS THE REWARD OF COURAGE.]
Lieutenant Colonel Frank Albro Creighton, 1st Battalion, June 16th 1916 (age 41)

Inside the hall of the Menin Gate. The list of the 6,983 Canadians killed in Flanders "to whom the fortune of war denied a known and honoured burial" begins on the panel immediately to the left of the portal.

IN MY LIFE WILL HIS REMEMBRANCE EVER LINGER.
Private Reginald Skidmore, 16th Battalion, June 17th 1916 (age 35)

YOU CANNOT PASS BEYOND OUR BOUNDLESS LOVE.
Private Kenneth Craig Corsan, 7th Battalion, June 19th 1916 (age 23)

HE DIED FOR THE RIGHT.
Private Alfred Wallace Geolot, 3rd Battalion, June 21st 1916 (age 22)

STEADFAST AND UNDAUNTED.
Gunner Harry Alfred Hadley, Canadian Field Artillery, June 22nd 1916 (age 20)

HE LOVED MUCH.
Private Hugh Lowell Hellings, Canadian Pioneers, June 23rd 1916

HE DIED AS HE LIVED, A SPORTSMAN.
Private Robert William Temple, 2nd Battalion, June 24th 1916 (age 28)

The transfer of the Canadians from the Ypres Salient to the Somme divides the war into two halves, a diptych inscribed on one panel with the placenames synonymous with Canada in Flanders, and on the other with those synonymous with the reputation of the Canadian Corps. The list on the first panel begins with a battle that remains a defining moment in Canadian history and ends with another that should be seen as a defining moment for the Canadian Corps. The surreal events of Second Ypres will never lose their dramatic force – the terrifying spectre of the gas cloud gusting towards them like a vision of death itself, the furious resistance amid panic and collapse, the agonizing realization that their rifles would not fire, the inexplicable courage and endurance of newly minted soldiers caught up in a first battle unlike any ever fought before, and the fallen immortalized on a scrap of paper tossed away and fortuitously retrieved and published. By contrast, the battle at Hill 62, or Sanctuary Wood, to put it in toponymic rather than cartographic terms, has faded in memory, but following upon two dismal reverses it restored the confidence of the Canadian Corps, and of others in it, and heralded the feats of arms to come.

GOD HATH CALLED YOU UNTO HIS KINGDOM AND GLORY.
Captain Robert Mansfield, Princess Patricia's Canadian Light Infantry, January 26th 1915 (age 30)

Opposite: View of Ypres from the Canadian memorial at Hill 62. This was the only significant high ground held by the Allies in the Salient in 1916 and its loss would likely have forced a withdrawal from Ypres, hence the Canadian efforts to take this ground back.

"GOD REST MY SOUL." THE LAST WORDS HE SAID.
Private Frances Guy Dwyer, Princess Patricia's Canadian Light Infantry, February 4th 1915 (age 20)

DUTY CALLED AND HE ANSWERED PROMPTLY.
Private Thomas Bruce Haddock, Princess Patricia's Canadian Light Infantry, February 28th 1915 (age 41)

1ST BATTN. THE SHERWOOD FORESTERS 1890-1911.
Major Percy George Rigby, 7th Battalion, March 10th 1915 (age 43)

HE SLEEPS AN IRON SLEEP, SLAIN FIGHTING FOR HIS COUNTRY.
Sergeant Thomas Patten DCM, Princess Patricia's Canadian Light Infantry, May 8th 1915 (age 39)

IF I FALL, I SHALL HAVE DONE SOMETHING WITH MY LIFE WORTH DOING.
Private George Lawrence Holmden, 5th Battalion, August 19th 1915

MORTUUS EST PRO SCOTIA.
[HE DIED FOR SCOTLAND.]
Lance Corporal Harry Walker, 29th Battalion, October 20th 1915 (age 24)

THROUGH MUCH TRIBULATION AT REST FROM ALL HIS LABOURS.
Private William Blissett, 3rd Battalion, November 8th 1915 (age 29)

NU LUKKER SIG MIT ØJE GUD FADER I DET HØJE I VARETÆGT MIG TAG.
[NOW MY EYES ARE CLOSED, DEAR FATHER, AND I ENTER THE CARE OF THE WORLD ABOVE.]
Private Count Ove Krag-Juel-Vind-Frijs, 28th Battalion, November 15th 1915 (age 25)

SCHOLAR, ATHLETE, CHRISTIAN SOLDIER. HE KNEW HIS DUTY AND HE DID IT.
Corporal George Gordon Galloway, Canadian Field Artillery, February 10th 1916 (age 21)

AND THUS THIS MAN DIED AN EXAMPLE OF NOBLE COURAGE. 2 MAC. VI. 31
Corporal John Ernest Lysle Millen, Princess Patricia's Canadian Light Infantry, February 19th 1916 (age 20)

THE FUTURE HOPE AND JOY OF THEIR YOUNG LIVES WERE SACRIFICED FOR US.
Private William Jeffery, 2nd Battalion, March 3rd 1916 (age 23)

WHO DIED FOR HIS KING AND COUNTRY AT THE TENDER AGE OF 17.
Private Frank Williams, 49th Battalion, April 14th 1916

Canadian headstones in Ploegsteert Wood Military Cemetery, at the southern tip of the Ypres Salient.

PAST THE MILITARY AGE, HE RESPONDED TO THE MOTHER COUNTRY'S CALL.
Regimental Sergeant Major Stewart Godfrey, Princess Patricia's Canadian Light Infantry, April 18th 1916 (age 47)

QUIT YOU LIKE MEN. BE STRONG. I COR. XVI. 13.
Lance Corporal Frank William Withers, Royal Canadian Regiment, May 25th 1916 (age 22)

A SPLENDID SON FOR WHOM NO PRAISE IS ADEQUATE.
Lance Corporal Douglas John Lamborn, Canadian Pioneers, June 30th 1916 (age 29)

The battlefield memorials distinguishing the actions designated as battles, as opposed to the daily exchange of hostilities, do only partial justice to the Canadians who served but did not survive their apprenticeship in Flanders. Dispersed among the 160 war cemeteries in the old Ypres Salient are the headstones of the soldiers claimed by the war, not in named battles but in scores of lesser actions and everyday incidents in the most lethal sector of the British front. Incessant artillery, snipers, mines, gas shells, random harassing fire, accidents, infections, and diseases all stalked the soldiers contending with the risks and foul conditions of trench life and getting through a day worse than the day before. What became all too commonplace in the salient, however, sent its ripples of shock and grief to faraway families, whose farewells gather into a memorial to the thousands of volunteers who fought and died in the place where the first chapter of Canada's Great War saga came to be written.

The three great mine craters blown by the Germans beneath the Canadian lines at Hooge in June of 1916 have since been landscaped into a pond and garden on the site of the Hooge Chateau (destroyed by artillery fire in 1915).

David Young Cameron *Flanders from Kemmel*
[CWM 19710261-0117 Beaverbrook Collection of War Art, Canadian War Museum]

111

4 HE FELL AT THE SOMME

The story of the Somme is etched into countryside, at first sight so serene as to defy belief that the battle whose very name encapsulates the horror of the First World War could have taken place there. Yet just as much part of the landscape as the chalk downlands, the ridges and valleys, the plateaus and woods, the monuments stand as silent witnesses to a tragedy played out in many places and felt in as many more. The villages studding the Old Front Line from Gommecourt to Montauban all display plaques twinning them with the communities in Britain home to the "Pals' battalions" – the young volunteers who hailed from the same towns, attended the same schools and churches, worked in the same factories and offices, belonged to the same clubs, played on the same football teams, and joined up together in the same local regiment – and whose decimation on July 1st, 1916 makes this the saddest day in British history. The two hundred and fifty war cemeteries on the Somme battlefield chart the devolution of an offensive intended to achieve a decisive breakthrough into a static attritional struggle that carried on for another four and a half months after its disastrous first day. By its end, the British and Dominion forces had made an advance of seven miles at its farthest point in return for 419,000 casualties. As with the other great hecatomb of 1916, Verdun, the Somme not only slew but obliterated its tens of thousands, bequeathing to posterity the largest of the monuments necessitated by the destructive powers of industrialized warfare, the daunting memorial to the missing at Thiepval, which records the names of the 73,000 soldiers never found or never identified. Although any judgment of the Somme must take the constricting realities of 1916 into account, it is hard when contemplating the "nameless names" of the missing or the *chaos humain* in the ossuary at Verdun not to wonder at the mentality of general staffs willing to trade ten lives for eleven, as though their men were merely disposable parts rather than human beings given to walk this way but once.

ONE OF CANADA'S BEST. NOW OUR MUCH LOVED DEAD.
Private John Wilson Aikens, 18th Battalion, September 15th 1916 (age 24)

"IT IS WELL DONE, DAD."
Private Richard Edgar Boughton, 21st Battalion, September 16th 1916 (age 41)

BELOVED SON, PROUD CANADIAN.
Private James Hayes, 24th Battalion, September 17th 1916 (age 18)

DÉCÉDÉ À LA BATAILLE DE COURCELETTE. A SA DOUCE MÉMOIRE.
[DIED IN THE BATTLE OF COURCELETTE. IN LOVING MEMORY.]
Private Emile Gascon, 22nd (French Canadian) Battalion, September 17th 1916 (age 19)

KILLED LEADING AN ATTACK AT REGINA TRENCH. LOYAL À MORT.
Lieutenant Willoughby Chatterton, 3rd Battalion, October 8th 1916 (age 26)

HE FELL AT THE SOMME. IT IS IMMORTAL HONOR.
Private James Edward Stickels, Royal Canadian Regiment, October 9th 1916 (age 18)

THIS CORNER OF A FOREIGN FIELD SHALL BE FOREVER CANADA.
Corporal Hugh Gordon Munro, 15th Battalion, October 9th 1916 (age 19)

LET THOSE WHO COME AFTER SEE TO IT THAT HIS NAME MAY NOT BE FORGOTTEN.
Private Robert Addison, 44th Battalion, October 25th 1916 (age 40)

ALSO HIS BROTHER CAPT. J.W.G. SMITH. KILLED 31ST AUGUST 1916.
Lieutenant Murray Turley Smith, 3rd Battalion, October 31st 1916 (age 25)

THE BETTER DAYS OF LIFE WERE OURS. THE WORST CAN BE BUT MINE.
Corporal Thomas Bourchier Cave, 102nd Battalion, November 11th 1916 (age 27)

HE SERVED HIS GENERATION.
Sergeant Peter Balfour Pennington, 73rd Battalion, November 13th 1916 (age 30)

DIED FOR KING AND COUNTRY WHILE KEEPING LINE OPEN UNDER SHELL FIRE.
Sergeant Harold Thomas Flynn, 38th Battalion, November 19th 1916 (age 21)

The Somme does not figure in Canadian memory of the Great War as prominently as it should, perhaps because the Canadians took no part in the first day's attack and were brought into the battle two months later. The memorial stone and garden at Courcelette honour the capture of the heavily fortified village by the 2nd and 3rd Canadian Divisions on September 15th, 1916, one of the few outright successes of the Somme campaign. The fields beyond, however, have their own tale to tell of the savage fighting that followed as the Canadians pressed on towards Regina Trench, a name ranking high in the sinister toponymy of the Somme. Four times in seven weeks, in the October rains and the November mud, the Canadian divisions were sent in turn to seize the long and shrewdly sited trenchline girding the enemy defences north of Courcelette, in an attempt to drive the Germans from their strong positions

Thurstan Topham *Trenches in the Chalk, the Somme*
[CWM 19710261-0731 Beaverbrook Collection of War Art, Canadian War Museum]

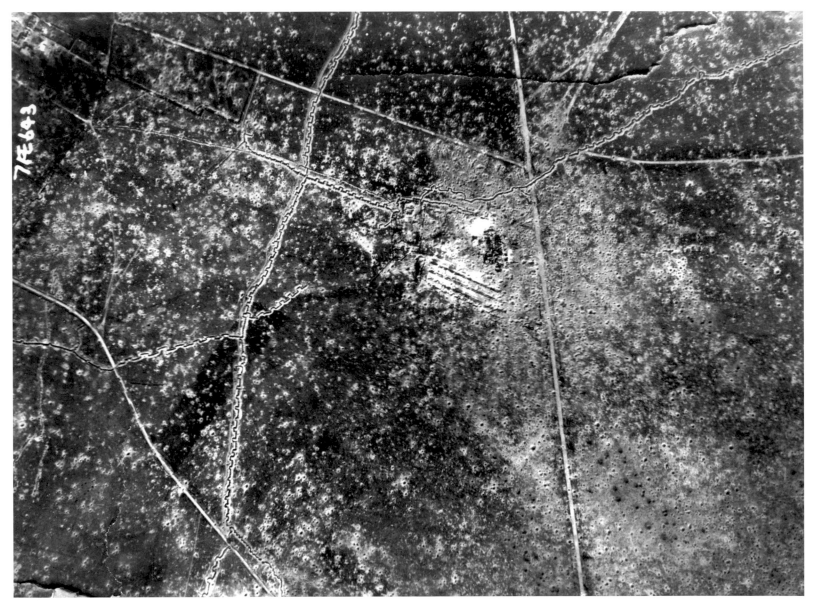

An aerial photograph showing the area of the sugar factory (immediately southwest of Courcelette) captured by the 2nd Canadian Division on September 15th, 1916. The trench line running from top to bottom was codenamed "Sugar Trench" by the Canadians. It intersected with "Candy Trench" to the left of the sugar factory. Six tanks accompanied the Canadian infantry battalions. The absence of tank tracks in the photo therefore suggests that it was taken shortly before the attack. The tanks and infantry started from the bottom of the photo and proceeded along the Albert–Bapaume road visible on the right.

dominating the centre of the battlefield. The death toll gives new meaning to the term "Pyrrhic victory." More than 7,300 British, Australian, and Canadian soldiers, the majority of them unidentified, lie in three large war cemeteries, one built astride the very trench so many had died to take, that mark out the scene of the longest, costliest, and most futile Canadian battle of the First World War. The rest are dispersed throughout another twenty-five of the Somme cemeteries. For a tract of ground traversed on foot in a couple of hours, the two and a half months of fighting necessary to claim it exacted 24,029 casualties (over 8,000 killed), a third again as many as Passchendaele, and left the Canadian Corps exhausted from a battle that it neither won nor lost, and from an experience its commanders were determined never to repeat.

Where Courcelette has faded in Canadian memory, however, Beaumont Hamel remains indelibly imprinted in the history of Newfoundland. So much of the role played by England's oldest and most loyal colony during the First World War is out of proportion to the island's relative size and population within the British Empire, be it the number of Newfoundlanders who served, their contribution on land and at sea, and the tragedy that befell the 1st Newfoundland Regiment on July 1st, 1916. Of the eight hundred men who went into the attack that morning, just sixty-eight answered the roll call the following day. Two hundred and forty-three were killed, the rest wounded, taken prisoner, or reported missing, although a number of these made it back to fight another day. Figures vary, but even the most cautious estimates point to a casualty rate of approximately 65% that even on a day strewn with disaster was exceeded by only one other regiment. It was the work of less than an hour.

O FRANCE, BE KIND AND KEEP GREEN FOR ME MY SOLDIER'S GRAVE. R.I.P. MOTHER
Private Robert John Williams, Royal Newfoundland Regiment, July 1st 1916 (age 21)

MY SON, YOU'RE NOT FORGOTTEN ALTHO' SO FAR AWAY.
Private John Frampton, Royal Newfoundland Regiment, July 1st 1916 (age 21)

The place where the Newfoundland Regiment made its ill-fated attack on July 1st has in recent years been transformed from a battlefield park into a well-tended and much visited memorial featuring the best-preserved trench lines on the old Somme battlefield. The centrepiece, of course, is the majestic sculpture of the caribou gazing out over the Newfoundlanders' line of advance. From the viewing stand below, the visitor can grasp at once the odds against the heavily laden infantrymen trudging down the slope towards the enemy front line, their chins tucked in as though walking into a blizzard at home, all the while profiled against the skyline and under full observation, hence aimed machine gun and artillery fire, from the rising ground beyond. What the mind's eye must supply are the thick nets of barbed wire in front of the British trenches through which the attackers had to pick their way before venturing into No Man's Land. So few and narrow were the gaps in the British wire that the men who got that far crowded fatally at points known and visible to the German machine gunners. The bodies of sixty-six men were later found at one such choked passageway. The focal point within this sobering panorama is the Danger Tree, where a replica marks the spot where a clump of shattered trees stood in No Man's Land. Barely a handful of men reached this forlorn landmark and the few who pushed on were mown down outside the German wire. It is likely that the defence of their front line cost the Germans not a single man. Nearly every Newfoundlander killed fell on ground held by the British before the attack began.

HE DIED IN THE SERVICE OF GOD AND HUMANITY.
Lieutenant Richard Shortall, Royal Newfoundland Regiment, July 1st 1916

BE ASHAMED TO DIE UNTIL YOU HAVE GAINED SOME VICTORY FOR HUMANITY.
Lance Corporal George Edward Pike, Royal Newfoundland Regiment, July 1st 1916 (age 33)

MY SON, MY SON, A CROWN THOU HAST WON OF EVERLASTING GLORY.
Private Michael John Holland, Royal Newfoundland Regiment, July 1st 1916 (age 19)

SOLDIER OF CHRIST, WELL DONE. REST IN THY SAVIOUR'S JOY.
Private John Snow, Royal Newfoundland Regiment, July 1st 1916

WHO DIED FOR KING AND COUNTRY. GOD'S WILL BE DONE.
Private Harry Butler, Royal Newfoundland Regiment, July 1st 1916 (age 20)

HE LOVED HONOUR MORE THAN HE FEARED DEATH.
Private Ernest Leslie Chafe, Royal Newfoundland Regiment, July 1st 1916 (age 25)

IT IS SWEET AND GLORIOUS TO DIE FOR ONE'S COUNTRY.
Private Wilson Bishop, Royal Newfoundland Regiment, July 1st 1916 (age 22)

HE DIED THAT HIS COUNTRY MIGHT LIVE.
Private Leo Michael Burke, Royal Newfoundland Regiment, July 1st 1916 (age 18)

GOOD IN LIFE, NOBLE IN DEATH, HE DIED FOR ME.
Private Donald Templeman, Royal Newfoundland Regiment, July 1st 1916 (age 23)

THOUGH WE MOURN HIM LET US NOT FORGET HIS IS A HERO'S GRAVE. MOTHER
Private Maxwell Janes, Royal Newfoundland Regiment, July 1st 1916 (age 20)

The Newfoundland Regiment advanced over this ground on July 1st 1916. The German front line ran through the ravine beyond the trees; the second line skirted the heights beyond. Y Ravine Cemetery contains 36 of the Newfoundlanders collected for burial nearly a year after the ill-fated attack.

The Danger Tree lent its name to a moving and memorable book tracing the war's impact on a single family and a whole society. For unlike the half British-born Canadian Corps, the Newfoundland Regiment was composed of native sons. The first day on the Somme proved as devastating to the colony as it did to the towns and villages in Britain left aghast at the losses and the realization that the war could rob them of a generation of young men whose desire to represent their kith and kin in the service of King and country had made them the pride of their communities. The disproportionate effect on a population as small as Newfoundland's can be gauged from the example of an extended family, the Ayres of St. John's, which lost two brothers and two cousins that morning,

moving – alone, exposed, unsupported, targets for every German gun within range. It is a wonder that any of them came out alive. The battlefield cemeteries where the Newfoundlanders now lie stand well short of the German line in mute testimony to a military disaster. The details on the headstones attest to the human consequences.

GOD KEEP THEE, MY SON, AND RIGHTLY BLESS THE LIFE THAT THOU HAST LAID DOWN.
Private Archibald Harold Porter, Royal Newfoundland Regiment, July 1st 1916 (age 21)

HIS NAME DEAR TO THE MEMORY OF FRIENDS.
Private Stanley Stewart Pinsent, Royal Newfoundland Regiment, July 1st 1916 (age 21)

GONE BUT NOT FORGOTTEN BY A MOTHER. MAY HIS SOUL REST IN PEACE.
Private Garland Warford, Royal Newfoundland Regiment, July 1st 1916 (age 22)

SLEEP ON, BELOVED, AND TAKE THY REST. MOTHER
Private Arthur Hayward, Royal Newfoundland Regiment, July 1st 1916 (age 22)

SLEEP ON, DEAR BELOVED, SLEEP. WE'LL MEET AGAIN, 'TWILL NOT BE LONG.
Private George Hawkins, Royal Newfoundland Regiment, July 1st 1916 (age 26)

WE SHALL GO TO HIM BUT HE SHALL NOT RETURN TO US.
Private George Stewart Small, Royal Newfoundland Regiment, July 1st 1916 (age 19)

UNTIL GOD RECKONS UP YOUR TALENTS, SOLDIER SLEEP, THY DUTY'S DONE.
Private Eric Shannon Martin, Royal Newfoundland Regiment, July 1st 1916 (age 23)

WE SHALL MEET AGAIN.
Private John Allan Jeans, Royal Newfoundland Regiment, July 1st 1916 (age 33)

UNTIL THE RESURRECTION MORN.
Lance Corporal John Herbert Hockley, Royal Newfoundland Regiment, July 1st 1916 (age 38)

"UNTIL THE DAY DAWN." II PETER I. 19
Private Reginald John Paul, Royal Newfoundland Regiment, July 1st 1916 (age 21)

The outlines of old trenches and redoubts are still visible on the Somme battlefields.

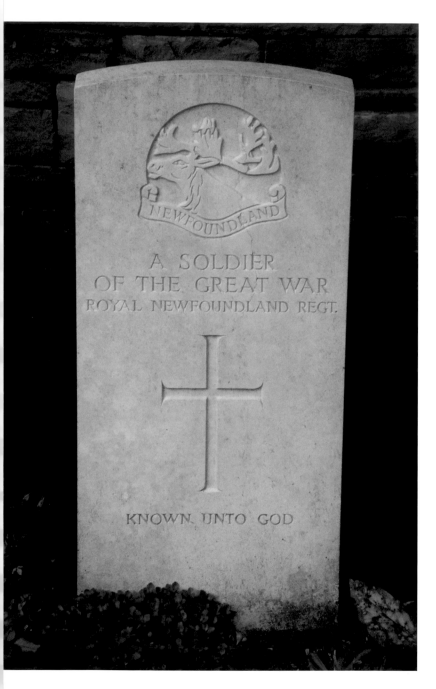

HE LEFT US TO FIGHT FOR TRUTH AND RIGHT.
Private Stephen Goodwin, Royal Newfoundland Regiment,
November 20th 1917 (age 21)

BENEATH THIS STONE A HERO SLEEPS
WHO GAVE HIS LIFE FOR HUMANITY.
Lieutenant Hedley John Goodyear MC, 102nd Battalion,
August 22nd 1918 (age 31)

WE LIVE IN DEEDS, NOT YEARS.
HE MOST LIVES WHO ACTS THE BEST.
Private Isaac John Snelgrove, Royal Newfoundland Regiment,
November 18th 1918 (age 22)

Skimming the lists of Newfoundland's fallen in the Great War, one is struck by the recurrence of names (Carew, Bennett, Dunphy, Janes, Clarke, Cleary, Butler, Reid, King) and what this implies about the wider effects of Beaumont Hamel and its sequels on a small and closely knit society. Reading the epitaphs in turn gives rise to the realization that, as in Britain, the sorrow was deepened by the belief that the war had taken the best of them. Newfoundland was a long time recovering from the First World War, financially and spiritually, saddled with a mountainous war debt that made the hard times of the 1920s and 1930s even harder, and deprived of a significant portion of any society's most vital asset, its young and their aspirations in life. Yet just as moving as the story of the Newfoundland Regiment is the fortitude of the bereaved who carried on, exemplified in *The Danger Tree*'s most sympathetic character, Kate Goodyear, who rarely spoke of her three lost brothers yet could never escape or conceal the pangs of grief that came unbidden all through her long and sturdy life.

Knightsbridge Cemetery profiled against the evening sky.

THE EVENING BRINGS ALL HOME.
Private Augustus Goodland, Royal Newfoundland Regiment, October 14th 1918 (age 18)

If the cross-section of fishermen, lumberjacks, tradesmen, students, seasonal labourers, shopkeepers, merchants, Catholics and Protestants, who filled the ranks of the Newfoundland Regiment shared one trait, it was that they did not want to be taken for Canadians – although it bears noting that over three thousand Newfoundlanders served in the CEF. What to outsiders was a remote, hardscrabble outpost of the British Empire was to its inhabitants and soldiers their country in all but name, with its own ways and traditions, and one more authentic and firmly rooted than the disparate miscellany of provinces and peoples next door. Whatever benefits accrued to Newfoundland upon joining Confederation in 1949, the mismatch nearly half of Newfoundlanders felt it to be could not have been more powerfully symbolized than by the coincidence of Canada's national day with the most heroic and terrible event in their history. The contrasting significance of July 1st is a reminder that the experience and the memory of the Great War reinforced an already strong sense of identity among Newfoundlanders and transformed the story of the Royal Newfoundland Regiment into an epic that was theirs and theirs alone. Of the many memorials honouring its place in the history of Newfoundland, perhaps none is more affecting than the heartfelt tributes to the young men missed and mourned all the more for their love of home and their service to a regiment epitomizing the pride and sorrow so closely entwined in the legacy of the Great War.

LOVED WE OUR COUNTRY MUCH, HE LOVED IT MORE.
Private Walter Norman, Royal Newfoundland Regiment, February 22nd 1917 (age 21)

AN OBEDIENT SON. A LOVING BROTHER. A LOVER OF KING AND NEWFOUNDLAND.
Private Nero Baker, Royal Newfoundland Regiment, February 3rd 1919 (age 26)

THIS SACRED DUST IS NEWFOUNDLAND, NOT FRANCE, AND HELD IN TRUST.
Corporal James Roy Tuff, Royal Newfoundland Regiment, April 28th 1917 (age 22)

Opposite: Two young visitors to Y Ravine Cemetery in the Newfoundland Memorial Park.

5 PASSCHENDAELE

The summer and fall of 2017 will bring centenaries of a campaign that resists explanation and beggars belief that the human frame and the human mind could endure its agonies. Passchendaele has become shorthand for the Third Battle of Ypres, a tragedy in eight acts that ran from July 31st to November 10th, 1917. It was the Somme re-enacted in Flanders, but on a smaller stage with four times the weight of artillery. Conceived as an ambitious offensive to crash through an enemy deemed to be at the breaking point, the campaign took three and a half months to reach its first-day objectives. By then it had degenerated into a crawl across the most hideous battlefield in history towards objectives blasted from the face of the earth and attained at a price out of all proportion to its purported tactical value. The sequel to Third Ypres underscores the gnawing question, never convincingly answered, of what greater end either side sought to achieve at such extortionate rates of return, other than its own incapacitation. Five months after the Canadian Corps completed the capture of the Passchendaele ridge, salvaging a modicum of success for a campaign that by its conclusion had cost the British and Dominion armies some 275,000 casualties, the British abandoned this hard-won ground without a fight when the Germans unleashed the second of their spring offensives. Judging the gains of Third Ypres to be untenable, the British withdrew to their original positions to fight Fourth Ypres along a stronger defensive line. One side simply turned the tables on the other, as now the Germans pressed their attacks across a sodden abattoir only to supplement the 220,000 casualties they had suffered there the year before. The outcome of the fighting hardly mattered – both sides could chisel away bits of defences thousands of yards in depth – but its intensity did, for it quickened the pace by which one side or the other exhausted its resources and resolve, all in a grim endurance contest easier to lose than to win.

KILLED NEAR PASSCHENDAELE.
Private Edward Francis Montagu Beldam, 2nd Canadian Mounted Rifles, October 30th 1917 (age 28)

ALSO IN MEMORY OF HIS BROTHER SAMUEL, KILLED AT COURCELETTE, 16TH SEPTEMBER 1916.
Private Alec William Feltham, 52nd Battalion, October 26th 1917 (age 21)

ALSO 2/LT. K.D. MURRAY 9/EAST SURREYS. THEY DIED FIGHTING FOR GOD & RIGHT & LIBERTY.
Sergeant Christopher Desmond Murray, 49th Battalion, October 30th 1917 (age 28)

ALSO IN MEMORY OF HIS BROTHER GILBERT, KILLED IN ACTION, PASSCHENDAELE.
Private Alex Duthie, 3rd Battalion, July 6th 1917 (age 23)

ALSO IN MEMORY OF PTE. HUGH BROWN MITCHELL,
28TH BN. CANADIAN INF., KILLED PASSCHENDAELE NOV. 17.
Private Hamilton Trelford Mitchell MM, 28th Battalion, May 12th 1918 (age 21)

FOR CANADA.
Private Edgar Ernest MacDonald, 52nd Battalion, November 14th 1917 (age 19)

Days after finishing the chore it had been brought in to do, the Canadian Corps took its dry-eyed leave of the Ypres Salient, never to return. To the death toll in Flanders, Passchendaele had added another 4,000 Canadians, half, like Private Edgar MacDonald above, to lie in marked graves, the rest, like his brother Private Walter MacDonald, killed the same day, to be listed among the missing on the Menin Gate or commemorated on the headstone of a brother killed elsewhere.

Ever afterwards, the name Passchendaele summoned up horrors all its own. More than any other battle, it corroded the physical and spiritual stamina of the soldiers who plodded through the Slough of Despond, inching their way forward over the viscid mud along narrow, slippery duckboards, magnets for enemy shells, past mangled corpses intimating the fate in store for them. The battle claimed men who had come through Sanctuary Wood, the Somme, or Vimy or Hill 70, and left the survivors wondering how much longer their luck would hold out. Nine Canadians won the Victoria Cross at Passchendaele, four on one day, in actions typifying the near suicidal heroism necessary to achieve even the smallest gains. No Canadian soldier huddled in the ruins of the village finally captured on November 10th, 1917, would have dreamt that the war had but a year and a day to run. If recent experience was any indication, his war would end with a shell blast or go on forever.

SURELY HE HATH BORNE OUR GRIEFS AND CARRIED OUR SORROWS. ISA. 53.4
Private William Budge, 78th Battalion, October 31st 1917 (age 29)

The panels forming the Tyne Cot Memorial complete the tally of the missing that begins on the Menin Gate.
They contain the names of 34,949 British soldiers listed as missing in the Ypres Salient after August 15, 1917.
Included are one Newfoundlander and one Canadian Victoria Cross winner from a British regiment.

WHO COMPREHENDS HIS TRUST AND TO THE SAME KEEPS FAITHFUL.
Lieutenant Bernard Coeure Montagnon MC, Canadian Machine Gun Corps, November 14th 1917 (age 29)
[William Wordsworth, "The Happy Warrior"]

A hundred years on, with the terms "duty" and "sacrifice" long in abeyance as a result of events such as Passchendaele, it is all but impossible to understand how men driven to the edge of sanity could persevere in such conditions. Granted, they had little choice in the matter, but ironclad rules and severe punishments did not keep other armies from buckling beneath the strain in 1917. Historians combing through the accounts and memoirs of the soldiers who fought at Passchendaele invariably come to the same answer, that no matter how frightened, tired, cynical, benumbed, or despairing they were, the majority gritted their teeth and stuck it out because their friends, their comrades, or even strangers in other units were counting on them. Loyalty, the fear of showing fear, the sense of shared risk and responsibility, comradeship, fidelity to friends and family, all contributed to the refusal to let the side down. If all did their jobs, more would survive. Skeleton crews of gunners manned their batteries round the clock despite constant enemy shelling and strafing in the knowledge that without their support the infantry would be massacred or overrun; to haul rations, tools, trench supplies, and ammunition forward, to carry the wounded back, to convey men into and out of the front line, the sappers, pioneers, and railway troops doggedly kept to their work even as the enemy gunners harassed them with gas shells and shrapnel. Nor should we discount sheer pride or stubbornness, since letting one's comrades down was also letting the Germans win and profaning the sacrifice that so many had already made.

HEAR, O GOD, SO WE BUILT THE WALL, FOR THE PEOPLE HAD A MIND TO WORK.
Gunner Edmund Holmes King, Canadian Field Artillery, October 19th 1917 (age 31)
[Nehemiah 4:6]

One of the five German bunkers enclosed within the precinct of Tyne Cot Cemetery.
Many of the Australian soldiers who died capturing it are buried close by.

The close interdependence of service units and fighting formations at Passchendaele, and the common exposure to danger, is particularly evident in the cross-section of casualties. With the evolution of the Canadian Corps' fighting methods, weaponry, and logistics came a growing reliance on the service corps, whose members as a result appear with greater frequency in the cemeteries from 1917 and 1918. Well before the Canadian drive on Passchendaele could begin, it was necessary to put the rear areas in working order by repairing the roads and light railways for mechanized transport, and laying corduroy tracks through the muddy wasteland to provide passage for the artillery and infantry. The headstones of the men who died performing these unsung yet vital tasks show many of them to have been somewhat older than the frontline soldiers, so that their epitaphs often take the form of farewells from wives and children. The instances of an epitaph in Italian and one in Czech (the latter echoing the nationalistic aspirations of a people longing to be free of Germany's Austro-Hungarian ally) are also revealing, since volunteers of non-British backgrounds – the native peoples, black Canadians, Eastern Europeans – tended for less than honourable reasons to be shunted into labour battalions and service corps. But on a battlefield under minute observation from the German side and well within reach of the German artillery behind the Passchendaele ridge, the support units, feeding the insatiable demands of their own infantry and artillery, drew their share of attention from enemy gunners and pilots attempting to disrupt the flow of men and supplies. Ten per cent of the Canadian casualties at Passchendaele belonged to the service corps working behind the lines.

ASLEEP WITH THE UNRETURNABLE BRAVE.
Sapper John Parsonage, Canadian Railway Troops, September 26th 1917 (age 31)

GONE BUT NOT FORGOTTEN. WIFE AND LITTLE SON
Sapper Matthew Donald, Canadian Railway Troops, September 27th 1917 (age 34)

HE DIED FOR THE HONOUR OF HIS COUNTRY.
Sapper Charles Branchfield, Canadian Railway Troops, October 5th 1917 (age 40)

EVEN AS THE FATHER HATH LOVED ME, I ALSO HAVE LOVED YOU. JOHN 15 V. 9.
Sapper Douglas Hanley Calhoun, Canadian Engineers, October 19th 1917 (age 27)

Alfred Bastien *Canadian Gunners in the Mud, Passchendaele*
[CWM 19710261-0093 Beaverbrook Collection of War Art, Canadian War Museum]

FROM MEMORY'S PAGE TIME CANNOT BLOT THREE LITTLE WORDS, FORGET ME NOT. R.I.P.
Corporal James Masterton, Canadian Machine Gun Corps, November 10th 1917 (age 27)

BELOVED ONLY SON, GONE HOME WITH HIS UNIFORM ON AND HIS DUTY DONE.
Gunner Edwin Roy Snow, Canadian Field Artillery, November 11th 1917 (age 34)

ONE WITH IMMORTAL LIFE THAT KNOWS NOT DEATH BUT EVER CHANGES FORM.
Lieutenant John Bain, Canadian Machine Gun Corps, November 11th 1917 (age 30)
[Lieutenant E.F. Wilkinson, "To My People, Before the Great Offensive," written June 30th, 1916]

IN THE EVENING AND THE MORNING WE WILL REMEMBER HIM.
Lieutenant Bernard Heath MC, Canadian Machine Gun Corps, November 11th 1917 (age 22)

TO THE GLORY OF HIS KINGDOM WHERE ALL TEARS ARE WIPED AWAY.
Private William Leo Gallery, Canadian Machine Gun Corps, November 11th 1917 (age 19)

BELOVED BY OFFICERS AND MEN.
Corporal George Basil Brown MM, Canadian Field Artillery, November 14th 1917 (age 30)

OUR ONLY BOY.
Gunner William James Coulter, Canadian Field Artillery, November 14th 1917 (age 21)

THE LORD SHALL PRESERVE THEE FROM ALL EVIL. HE SHALL PRESERVE THY SOUL. PSALM 121, 7TH VERSE.
Gunner Herbert Edward Shipton, Canadian Garrison Artillery, November 16th 1917 (age 19)

The infantry assault is a story in three chapters with a brief epilogue. The Canadians were attacking a horseshoe whose arms were ridges separated by a shallow valley described on the memorial at Passchendaele as a "treacherous morass." The defenders were ensonced not in a fixed trench system – too inflexible, too obvious a target for artillery, and too difficult to maintain in the waterlogged terrain – but in a dispersed, mutually supporting network of machine gun nests, pillboxes, and bunkers fronted by thickets of barbed wire. Some of this the artillery could deal with, cutting the wire and keeping the enemy's heads down, but the barrage was also a calling card serving notice of the infantry's arrival. It was best to leave little time in between if the attackers were to isolate and neutralize the resistance points before the defenders recovered and responded. Even in the most meticulously planned and coordinated attacks, errors, surprises, emergencies, and enemy reactions, for which no one could plan, intervened, at which point the initiative and courage

Opposite: A view of Passchendaele showing the narrow stream of the Ravebeek (marked by the line of trees)
and the high ground to the right. Crest Farm would have been just on the other side of the trees on the right.

of a single soldier, or of a handful of men, decided the issue. The fighting around the critical Bellevue Spur and Decline Copse saw a number of brave pivotal acts, some recognized and commended, others regarded as a matter of course, on the part of sergeants, corporals, and privates who tilted the balance ever so slightly in favour of their comrades.

"WHO WAS FAITHFUL TO HIM THAT APPOINTED HIM." HEB. 3. 2
Private Frederick Stanley Albright, 50th Battalion, October 26th 1917 (age 34)

SOWN IN WEAKNESS, RAISED IN POWER.
Corporal David Stewart MM, 43rd Battalion, October 26th 1917 (age 25)
[I Corinthians 15:43]

ENLISTED MAR. 11-1916 AT EDMONTON, ALBERTA. KILLED IN ACTION.
Private George Walter McLean, 50th Battalion, October 26th 1917 (age 32)

WOULD SOME THOUGHTFUL HAND IN THIS DISTANT LAND PLEASE SCATTER SOME FLOWERS FOR ME.
Private Edwin Grant, 47th Battalion, October 26th 1917 (age 33)

HE DIED FOR FREEDOM AND HONOR.
Private William Laird, 44th Battalion, October 26th 1917 (age 25)

MY SON, I LOVED YOU SO DEARLY.
MY DEEPEST SORROW CAN NEVER BE HEALED. MOTHER
Lance Sergeant Joseph Johnston, 43rd Battalion, October 26th 1917 (age 26)

THE DEAD GAVE US FREEDOM.
Private Walter Holmes Baker, 46th Battalion, October 27th 1917 (age 18)

BRIEF, BRAVE, AND GLORIOUS WAS HIS YOUNG CAREER.
Private Hugh Chester Blackmore, 46th Battalion, October 27th 1917 (age 23)

HE ALLURED TO BRIGHTER WORLDS AND LED THE WAY.
Company Sergeant Major Arthur Dunlop, 4th Canadian Mounted Rifles, October 27th 1917 (age 30)
[Oliver Goldsmith, "The Deserted Village"]

Opposite: The long path leading to the memorial honouring the 12 officers and 132 other ranks of the 85th Battalion (Nova Scotia Highlanders) killed in the advance on Passchendaele in late October of 1917. Recently restored, it was the only battalion memorial put up by the comrades of the fallen before the end of the war.

THEIR GRAVES ARE ALTARS. HONOR AND PRAISE BUT MOURN THEM NOT.
Major Ralph Russell James Brown, 44th Battalion, October 31st 1917 (age 42)

Seizing the tips of the horseshoe and gaining five hundred yards of less intractable ground had cost the attackers 2,481 casualties. A similar ratio would apply to the next bound forward, this time covering about a thousand yards to secure a line for the final assault on the village and the crest of the ridge. Source Farm, Vapour Farm, Meetchele, Snipe Hall, Graf Wood, Crest Farm, Vienna Cottage, each a formidable redoubt in the chain of German defences barring the way, were obstacles that could be overcome only by companies and platoons improvising in reaction to the unknown and the unforeseen. In devising an attack through waist-deep mud where every new shellhole might house a machine-gun crew and landmarks existed in name only, the high command could formulate none but the loosest of plans and leave the fine print to their junior officers and NCOs. The barrages were adjusted to lead the slowest charge in history, according to one participant, while the first wave had to carry a good deal more ammunition, rations, and tools than normal to fend for itself, since resupply would be a long time coming. Yet once again, the soldiers showed that the trust invested in them was not misplaced, even as the second instalment on Currie's estimate came due.

MENTIONED IN DESPATCHES. YOUR MEMORY HALLOWED IN THE LAND YOU LOVED.
Lieutenant Allan Otty, 5th Canadian Mounted Rifles, October 30th 1917 (age 29)

THEY SHALL SEE HIS FACE AND HIS NAME SHALL BE IN THEIR FOREHEADS.
REV. 22 CH. 4TH VERSE
Lance Corporal James Warren Davidson, 85th Battalion, October 30th 1917 (age 22)

LEAVING A LONELY WIFE AND CHILD.
Private Francis James Sinclair, 72nd Battalion, October 30th 1917 (age 32)

THUG THU BARRACHD ANN AM BEUS.
[YOU WERE SURPASSING IN VIRTUE.]
Private Hugh MacInnes, 72nd Battalion, October 30th 1917 (age 24)

A frosty morning at Crest Farm Memorial, Passchendaele

The Victoria Cross engraved on the headstones of an Australian and a Canadian soldier buried in Tyne Cot attests to their courage, and to the courage of their comrades, in a battle synonymous with the horrors of the First World War.

HE WORE THE WHITE FLOWER OF A BLAMELESS LIFE.
Private Edgar Brierley, 7th Battalion, November 10th 1917 (age 35)

WE WILL REMEMBER WHEN OTHERS FORGET. WIFE AND DAUGHTER
Private Edward William Covington, 7th Battalion, November 10th 1917 (age 39)

I THANK MY GOD FOR EVERY REMEMBRANCE OF YOU.
Sapper Charles Forrest Patterson, Canadian Signal Corps, November 13th 1917 (age 21)

The Canadians at Passchendaele had done everything asked of them. Whereas at Vimy many had gone into battle with the belief that they were writing a significant chapter in Canadian history, or at Amiens the following year, where the feeling ran high that the decisive moment was now at hand, victory at Passchendaele offered no obvious recompense for the price necessary to achieve it or for the sorrows it inflicted. The soldiers had upheld the reputation of the Canadian Corps and had, with their considerable assistance, redeemed the efforts and sacrifice of their British, Australian, and New Zealand comrades, at least in some measure; but if there is any consensus about Second Passchendaele, it is that this battle need never have been fought. But it was, and of all the Canadian battles fought on the Western Front, it deserves commemoration not as a feat of arms, though that it was, but as a testament to the soldiers who did their duty and saw the struggle through to the end, bringing honour to their country and eliciting from a later generation a profound sympathy for their suffering and admiration for their fortitude. Their endurance has a simple grandeur about it that gives the Canadians who fought and died at Passchendaele a place apart in the national memory of the First World War.

STEADFAST IN LIFE, VALIANT IN DEATH.
Lance Corporal Thomas Grayburn, 42nd Battalion, November 3rd 1917 (age 21)

WORDS FAIL TO ADD ANYTHING TO THE HONOR
OF OUR GLORIOUS DEAD.
Private Clifford Waterworth Baskerville, 1st Canadian Mounted Rifles,
November 14th 1917 (age 27)

WHAT GREATER THING THAN THIS COULD MAN HAVE DONE. EVER REMEMBERED.
Lance Corporal William Henry Hawkins, 31st Battalion, November 6th 1917 (age 37)

A memorial recording the names of 378 New Zealand soldiers listed among the missing at Passchendaele and later battles stands in Buttes New British Cemetery. Shrouded by Polygon Wood, the burial ground includes five Canadians among the 2,108 British and Dominion graves.

6 THE HUNDRED DAYS

So strong is the hold of the Somme or Passchendaele on the popular memory of the First World War that its result in an Allied victory is often minimized. There is an understandable tendency to regard the war in the light of the human loss and the still greater tragedy that ensued twenty years later, and hence to overlook the importance of the victory as contemporaries saw it. Distance gives perspective, but it can also obscure as much as clarify the past, and it is easy today to lose sight of the vindication that Canadians felt upon receiving word of the Armistice. The leading part the country's soldiers had played in the last hundred days of the war put the jewel in the crown of the Canadian Corps, which in four major operations had accomplished the most elusive of Great War objectives, delivering a series of mortal blows that shattered the enemy's defences and eroded his will to resist. Aside from the moral and religious meaning attached to the final victory, already much emphasized, the disproportionate Canadian contribution to the defeat of the German army served the necessary military and political purposes in denying a beaten enemy the chance for a negotiated settlement and forcing him to relinquish the French and Belgian territory occupied since 1914 – the *sine qua non* among the Allied war aims. It is worth remembering that the Canadians who entered Cambrai and Valenciennes and Mons in 1918 met the same jubilant reception as would their sons during a second liberation twenty-six years later.

HE TOOK THE ONLY WAY & FOLLOWED IT TO A GLORIOUS END.
Lieutenant Peter Robert Swann MM, 20th Battalion, August 8th 1918 (age 23)

VINCIT QUI PATITUR.
[HE WHO ENDURES WINS.]
Major Thomas Duncan John Ringwood, Canadian Field Artillery, August 10th 1918 (age 31)

With so little opportunity for manoeuvre or breakthrough, the war was an endurance contest to be decided as much by the willingness of the home front to bear the strain of the war effort as by the staying power of the armies. After so much unrewarded effort and so many false dawns, the war-weary Canadian public reacted cautiously at first to the reports of the great gains and advances their soldiers were making. Even as the implications of these victories began to sink in, the distressing casualty lists restrained the growing excitement that the war would soon come to its long-awaited conclusion. The Canadian Corps' greatest triumphs were also its most costly, starting with more than a thousand dead on the decisive "eighth of the eighth" and ending with the death of Private George Lawrence Price moments before the Armistice came into effect. Between August 8th and November 11th, some 45,000 Canadians, one in six of all the country's Great War losses, were killed or wounded, many of the latter to succumb to their wounds or influenza in the first days and months of peace. Little wonder that most soldiers seem to have responded to the Armistice with subdued emotions, while many at home, after an initial outburst of celebration, turned pensive and introspective as they slowly realized how much the war had taken out of them. If any feeling was universal, it was relief, for the victory had ended a war that until the fall of 1918 had shown every sign of continuing well into 1919 or even 1920. Liberated from that grim prospect, the nation proud of the achievements of the Canadian Corps felt an even deeper sense of gratitude at being relieved of a burden that it could not have borne much longer.

DEATH IS SWALLOWED UP IN VICTORY. MEMORIA IN AETERNA.
Lieutenant Kingsley Spencer, 52nd Battalion, August 8th 1918 (age 23)
[I Corinthians 15:54 / In everlasting memory]

BLESSED ARE THE DEAD WHO DIE IN THE LORD AND FOR VICTORY'S CAUSE.
Private Charles Hedley Fulton, Royal Canadian Regiment, August 8th 1918 (age 19)
[Revelation 14:13]

Victory, with the much needed consolation and hopes it brought, was embraced all the more closely, since the decision had very nearly gone the other way short months before. In a bid to win the war outright or dictate a peace settlement on their terms before the arrival of the Americans tipped the scales too heavily against them, the Germans unleashed four major offensives between March and May of 1918 that came within a hair's breadth of success. But having shot their bolt and missed, the Germans had left themselves in a highly precarious position. Their waning armies now held a weaker front far in advance of the deep and heavily fortified defensive zone they had built up over the previous two years. They had ceded the momentum to the Allies now waxing in strength and numbers, and whose armies could now gather for a massive counteroffensive to be spearheaded by its two ablest attacking formations, the Canadians and Australians. The Canadian Corps was rested and ready, its morale high, and its soldiers aware that the moment had come to strike the decisive blow.

TOMORROW WILL BE CANADA'S DAY.
Lieutenant Colonel Elmer Watson Jones DSO and Bar, 21st Battalion, August 8th 1918 (age 44)

A view over Veillers-Bretonneux Military Cemetery from the Australian National Memorial. The great victory on August 8th, 1918, was the work of many hands, and so it is fitting that the 267 Canadians buried here lie alongside their British, Australian, and New Zealand comrades-in-arms.

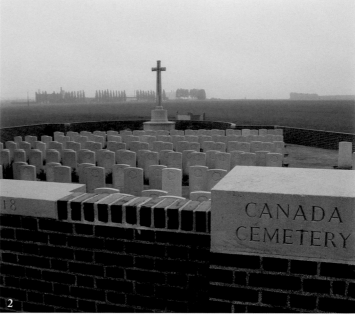

The Canadian achievements in the Hundred Days echo in the names of the cemeteries housing the fallen:

1 – Niagara Cemetery, east of Cambrai

2 – Canada Cemetery, on the western edge of Cambrai

3 – Quebec Cemetery, east of Arras

4 – Toronto (Demuin), southest of Amiens.

I WILL BE EQUAL TO ANY DUTY REQUIRED OF ME NO MATTER WHAT IT COSTS.
Private Robert Doyle, Canadian Machine Gun Corps, August 8th 1918 (age 25)

The flat, open landscape east of Amiens, where the Canadians launched their first great attack, is speckled with small woods and villages that became the scenes of fierce fighting during the longest single-day advance made by any British or Dominion force during the war. An archipelago of battlefield cemeteries taking their names from local landmarks (Hangard Wood, Démuin, Caix, Fouquescourt, Roye) or echoing distant homes (Toronto, Manitoba) stretches eight miles from the Canadian start line and charts each day's progress from August 8th to August 14th. To friend and foe alike, Amiens signalled the beginning of the end, as the unprecedented scale of the Allied success and the hordes of prisoners gave every reason to believe. Though a remarkable success, it was in truth a sizable dent, not a breakthrough, and the operation was sensibly called off once the ratio of losses to ground gained reverted to the Great War norm. And though the now highly professional Canadian Corps employed the full panoply of artillery, tanks, motorized units, and aircraft, the outcome rested on the skills and courage of the infantry, amply demonstrated in the seven Victoria Crosses won on the first day alone and in the fearsome risks they knowingly faced. Of the 12,000 casualties at Amiens, eight in every ten were the men who went open-eyed into the attack, trying to keep their minds on the task before them rather than on the odds against them.

DO YOU WISH TO SHOW YOUR GRATITUDE? KNEEL DOWN AND PRAY FOR MY SOUL.
Private John Bernard Croak VC, 13th Battalion, August 8th 1918 (age 26)

OUR LAD IS A HERO, GREAT CANADA'S PRIDE. FOR GLORY HE DIED.
Private Wilfrid Robert Spicer, 2nd Battalion, August 8th 1918 (age 21)

HE DIED FIGHTING FOR THE COUNTRY HE LOVED SO MUCH.
Private Harry Fentiman, 15th Battalion, August 8th 1918 (age 20)

FAITHFUL & TRUE, HE VOLUNTARILY DID HIS DUTY FOR GOD & COUNTRY.
Private Frederick Compton Lawes, 4th Battalion, August 8th 1918 (age 21)

SORROW VANQUISHED, LABOUR ENDED, JORDAN PASSED.
Private William Armstrong Syer, 2nd Canadian Mounted Rifles, August 8th 1918 (age 34)

THE LIGHT OF OUR HOUSEHOLD GONE. GONE BUT NOT FORGOTTEN. FROM WIFE & CHILDREN
Private Henry Butler, 18th Battalion, August 8th 1918 (age 35)

DORS, JEAN PAUL, DANS UN DOUX SOMMEIL. LA CROIX GARDERA TA DEMEURE.
[SLEEP, JEAN PAUL, IN GENTLE SLUMBER. THE CROSS WILL STAND OVER YOUR RESTING PLACE.]
Private Jean Paul Grignon MM, 75th Battalion, August 9th 1918 (age 26)

THE WIND OF DEATH FOR YOU HAS SLAIN LIFE'S FLOWERS.
Private Wellington Murray Dennis, 5th Battalion, August 9th 1918 (age 24)

WHO LOVED ME AND GAVE HIMSELF FOR ME. GAL. 2. 20
Private Arthur Edward Doxsee, 68th Battalion, August 9th 1918 (age 22)

HIS LABOUR DONE, THE GREAT VICTORY WON. LET OUR BELOVED SLEEP.
Private Gordon Mitchell Spence, 1st Battalion, August 9th 1918 (age 28)

IMMORTAL SEED IN GLORIOUS SOIL, RISE AND BLOOM ON HIGH.
Private Edward Leon Mason, 72nd Battalion, August 9th 1918 (age 18)

FILS DE JOSEPH BRILLANT. ENROLÉ VOLONTAIREMENT À RIMOUSKI, PROVINCE DE QUÉBEC.
TOMBÉ GLORIEUSEMENT SUR LE SOL DE SES AÏEUX. BON SANG NE PEUT MENTIR.
[SON OF JOSEPH BRILLANT. ENLISTED VOLUNTARILY AT RIMOUSKI, PROVINCE OF QUEBEC.
FELL GLORIOUSLY ON THE SOIL OF HIS FOREFATHERS. A NOBLE NATURE CANNOT PLAY FALSE.]
Lieutenant Jean Brillant VC, 22nd (French Canadian) Battalion, August 10th 1918 (age 28)

HE DID NOT SHIRK THE POST ALLOTTED BY THE GODS.
Corporal James Crickmore Craig, Canadian Machine Gun Corps, August 10th 1918 (age 26)

DIED IN EFFORT TO RESCUE A WOUNDED COMRADE.
Private George Crawford Dale, 47th Battalion, August 10th 1918 (age 21)

HONOUR THE MEMORY OF CANADA'S BRAVEST AND BEST.
Private Isaac William Jones, 116th Battalion, August 10th 1918 (age 22)

BRAVEST OF THE BRAVE, TRUEST OF THE TRUE, WHO FREELY GAVE HIS LIFE WHEN LIFE WAS SWEETEST.
Private Hugh Gillies, 2nd Canadian Mounted Rifles, August 11th 1918 (age 25)

A LIFE GIVEN FREELY FOR THE WORLD HE DIED TO SAVE. MOTHER
Private Arthur Gerald Godwin, 8th Battalion, August 12th 1918

HE DIED LIKE A MAN BUT FELL LIKE A PRINCE. MOTHER
Private Clyde Emerson Stout, 3rd Battalion, August 15th 1918 (age 23)

Maurice Cullen *The Sunken Road, Hangard*
[CWM 19710261-0127 Beaverbrook Collection of War Art, Canadian War Museum]

Alfred Bastien *Over the Top, Neuville-Vitasse*
[CWM 19710261-0056 Beaverbrook Collection of War Art, Canadian War Museum]

The 8th of August has gone down as the "black day of the German army," but even in the tide of its advance the Canadian Corps was to know harsh days of its own. Rather than sue for peace after Amiens, as they ought to have done, the Germans played for time by retiring into the labyrinthine depths of the Hindenburg Line, east of Arras, there to fight the Allies to a bloody standstill and at least escape defeat. The sector assigned to the Canadians could be described as an obstacle course more than ten miles deep, composed of interlocking trenchworks, machine-gun nests, and belts of barbed wire, all engineered with the rise and fall of the terrain. To break through the strongest defences the Germans ever built on the Western Front, unhinge their last defensive system, and extinguish any hope of a settlement on equal terms, the Canadians had four days to prepare for their hardest and most decisive battle of the war. It would prove a victory greater than Vimy. Yet of this battle hardly a trace remains today. The granite block at Dury stands on the Drocourt-Quéant Line, the linchpin of the vaunted Hindenburg Line, which has long since been returned to the plough. The memory endures in Ontario Cemetery, Quebec Cemetery, Dominion Cemetery, Canada Cemetery – islands of remembrance in another archipelago along the road from Arras to Cambrai, where the headstones preserve the testimony to the soldiers who fell in a battle hailed as the turning point in the Allied campaign.

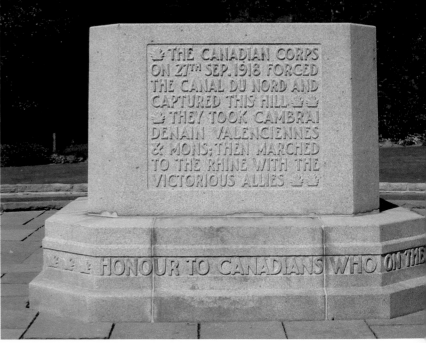

Left: The Canal du Nord today. The Canadians crossed an unfinished section astride the road between Arras and Cambrai.
Right: The memorial at Bourlon Wood that records the Canadian feats of arms in the final weeks of the war.

AFTER ME SORROW DO NOT TAKE BUT LOVE EACH OTHER FOR MY SAKE.
Private Louis Narcis Harris, Canadian Machine Gun Corps, August 26th 1918 (age 22)

SO HE BRINGETH THEM UNTO THEIR DESIRED HAVEN. PS. CVII. 30
Private James Newell Leighton, 29th Battalion, August 27th 1918 (age 23)

TO ALL HUMAN FEARS, TO SUFFERING OF EVERY SORT, PEACE BE STILL.
Private Herbert Anthony Maxey, 25th Battalion, August 27th 1918 (age 25)

DEATH AND TIME SHALL NEVER OBLITERATE HIS NOBLE MEMORY.
Private Leon Andrew Delauney, 116th Battalion, August 27th 1918 (age 17)

POUR SA PATRIE IL A DONNÉ SA JEUNESSE ET SA VIE.
[FOR HIS COUNTRY HE GAVE HIS YOUTH AND HIS LIFE.]
Lance Sergeant Dalvaine Lamarche, 22nd (French Canadian) Battalion, August 27th 1918 (age 20)

I GAVE MY BODY TO THE EARTH, MY SOUL TO GOD, AND MY HEART TO HUMANITY.
Private Arthur Garfield Swalles, Canadian Machine Gun Corps, August 29th 1918 (age 20)

SLEEP, MY LOVE, AND PEACE ATTEND THEE. OH, WITHOUT THEE WHAT AM I, LADDIE? (LILY)
Private Thomas Henry Bocking, 4th Canadian Mounted Rifles, August 29th 1918 (age 23)

I WILL TRUST AND NOT BE AFRAID.
Private Frederick Harold Croydon, 58th Battalion, August 29th 1918 (age 19)
[Isaiah 12:2]

A FAITHFUL HUSBAND, A TRUE PATRIOT, AND A BRAVE SOLDIER OF HIS COUNTRY.
Private William Henry Dine, 1st Battalion, August 30th 1918 (age 34)

HE WAS A GOOD SON & DEVOTED TO HIS MOTHER.
Lieutenant Burnett Grosvenor, 3rd Battalion, August 30th 1918 (age 26)

NOT A SORROW OR A JOY BUT WE LONG TO CALL THEE BACK. TILL WE MEET.
Signaller Leslie James Scott, 28th Battalion, August 30th 1918 (age 20)

PEACE, PERFECT PEACE. HE DID KEEP FAITH. THE MAPLE LEAF FOREVER.
Lance Sergeant James Shepard, 15th Battalion, September 1st 1918 (age 25)

His life was not ours to keep. God and his country called him.
Lance Corporal Ernest Baden Powell Davies, 54th Battalion, September 30th 1918 (age 20)

Valiant in battle.
Lieutenant George Cecil Kearsley MM, 75th Battalion, September 30th 1918 (age 27)

Killed in action at Cambrai. I shall go to him, but he shall not return.
Private William Campbell Bartling, 52nd Battalion, October 1st 1918 (age 30)

Battalion runner. Short life well spent.
Private Robert Lunn, 16th Battalion, October 1st 1918 (age 28)

O Canada, he stood on guard for thee.
Private Reginald George Box, 16th Battalion, October 1st 1918 (age 24)

Baby of the family. Born Green Bay, Wisc. U.S.A.
Mother still anxious for his return.
Private Albert Kick, 4th Battalion, October 1st 1918 (age 29)

Not since her birth has our earth seen such worth loosed upon it.
Lance Sergeant Alexander Lorimer Riddell, 54th Battalion, October 3rd 1918 (age 33)

He shall return no more to his house; neither shall his place know him any more. Job 7.10.
Private Maurice Singer, 24th Battalion, October 5th 1918 (age 20)

For God, King and country (Boy Scout oath).
Gunner Archibald Edward Ford, Canadian Field Artillery, October 8th 1918 (age 19)

He died as he lived, helping the weak.
Private John Kirk Fergus, Canadian Corps Cyclist Battalion, October 10th 1918 (age 26)

The Lord deal kindly with you as you have dealt with me.
Private Henry John Parkins, 21st Battalion, October 11th 1918 (age 25)

The war cemeteries between Cambrai and Mons are perhaps the saddest of all. They contain the graves of the men who came within days and hours of surviving the war but were killed doing their duty to the very end. Even with the outcome no longer in doubt, the fighting carried on to the appointed hour. The Allied commanders believed that it was necessary to keep the pressure on the Germans

Bourlon Wood Cemetery, where 221 Canadian soldiers lie at rest.

One of the two Canadian soldiers buried in St. Symphorien Military Cemetery, just east of Mons, is Private George Price, who was killed moments before the Armistice came into effect. Not far away are the graves of the first British soldiers to be killed in the Great War.

and to advance as far as possible in case the enemy attempted to prolong the war into 1919 or to use an armistice as a moratorium. Any armistice, when it came, would have to be treated as a ceasefire, not as a surrender or a definitive end to the war. The Canadians pushed on, cautiously but persistently, towards the town where, by quirk of fate, the British Empire's war had begun and where, on November 11th, the guns at last fell silent.

THE PASSING OF HIS LIFE LEFT A SORROW FAR AND WIDE.
Major Atwood Talbot MacKay DSO, Canadian Field Artillery, October 26th 1918 (age 34)

LET IT NOT BE IN VAIN THAT THOU HAST DIED.
Sapper David Lloyd, Canadian Engineers, October 31st 1918 (age 34)

LO, THE PAIN OF LIFE IS PAST. ALL HIS WARFARE NOW IS O'ER.
Private John Stanley Malzard, 19th Battalion, November 10th 1918 (age 31)

There are epitaphs that compress the pathos of the war into a single line. One such is found on a grave in Mons, in St. Symphorien Cemetery where the first and last British and Dominion soldiers killed in the Great War lie at rest. In a place so symbolic, where the circle finally closed, nine words on a British grave capture the tragedy of a generation and the magnitude of the loss that the survivors were left to address.

THESE WHO DESIRED TO LIVE WENT OUT TO DEATH.
Lieutenant John Rothes Marlow Wilkinson, Middlesex Regiment, August 23rd 1914 (age 26)

With the fighting over, the war's last tasks remained, to commemorate the fallen and to comfort the mourners. The consoling ideals of duty and patriotism, of redemption through sacrifice, and the belief that the Glorious Dead had given their lives in a necessary and worthy cause, have found manifold expression in these pages. This was to remember the fallen as soldiers and to honour their record from the heroic stand at Second Ypres to the triumph of the Hundred Days. Pride in their military achievements, coupled with gratitude for their resolute defence of democratic and Christian principles, was a crucial element of consolation that victory had offered; and we may well wonder how much more devastating the impact of loss would have been, or what answers bereaved Canadians could have sought, had the Allies not prevailed in the struggle. But the generation that was the first to suffer the effects of modern war had also been raised in an era of progress that had given parents, for the first time in history, reason to expect that their children would safely outlive them. The reversal of their expectations, and the emptiness it left in so many lives, drew the bereaved to another form of consolation, common before the war but much more enticing in the years that followed. To people remembering the fallen as their children, or as young men cut down in the prime of life, it offered a tranquil image of death as the gateway from this dark world of sin to "that far land of peace and joy," and as a release from the strife and torments of war. We should not be surprised that a populace passing from war to peace would wish to project a similar transition onto the fallen and soften the blow of loss with the consoling thought that those they loved and missed awaited them in a better world.

MY DARLING BOY. AT PEACE AFTER WAR. MOTHER
Private Roy Sanderson, 27th Battalion, December 15th 1917 (age 27)

NO LONGER DOES THE HELMET PRESS THY BROW, OFT WEARY WITH ITS SURGING THOUGHTS OF BATTLE.
Sergeant William McEwan, 2nd Battalion, September 15th 1916 (age 27)

FOREVER DONE WITH SWORD AND CONFLICT WHERE ALL IS CALM AND BRIGHT.
Private Henry Horwood, Royal Newfoundland Regiment, October 20th 1918 (age 23)

TRANSPLANTED BY HIS FATHER'S CARE TO FAIRER WORLDS ABOVE.
Private Fred Gordon McNeil, 46th Battalion, May 1st 1917 (age 20)

TAKEN AWAY FROM THE EVIL TO COME.
Private Hugh McCabe, 14th Battalion, November 4th 1915 (age 26)

FROM THE CONTAGION OF THE WORLD'S SLOW STAIN HE IS SECURE.
Private William John May, 38th Battalion, January 3rd 1917 (age 21)
[Percy Bysshe Shelley, "Adonais"]

HE HAS GONE ON HIS LAST COMMISSION TO THAT BEAUTIFUL PLACE CALLED REST.
Captain Harry Whiteman, 10th Battalion, April 1st 1916 (age 37)

THERE IS NO DEATH. WHAT SEEMS SO IS TRANSITION TO A HIGHER LIFE.
Private Leonard Endicott, 2nd Battalion, April 25th 1916 (age 26)

THERE IS A CALM BEYOND LIFE'S FITFUL FEVER.
Corporal John Smith Ross, Canadian Pioneers, September 27th 1916 (age 27)
[Hymn, "There Is a Calm"]

CLOSE UPON THE FIELD OF STRIFE OPEN STANDS THE GATE OF LIFE.
Private Alastair Fraser, 47th Battalion, March 31st 1917 (age 32)

NO MORE SORROW, NO MORE WEEPING, NO MORE PAIN.
Corporal Frank Jancey MM, 4th Battalion, August 22nd 1918 (age 22)

Maurice Cullen *The Cambrai Road*
[CWM 19880266-002 Beaverbrook Collection of War Art, Canadian War Museum]

7
HE SLEEPS NOT HERE
BUT IN HEARTS ACROSS THE SEAS

This chapter offers a selection of Canadian epitaphs as one might chance upon them in a war cemetery. They echo the themes touched on in previous chapters, but they also stand out for their particularity or memorable effect and thus give the reader pause for reflection. And just as the Great War cemeteries often include German graves, we have presented a number of images showing cemeteries and headstones of various nationalities, both to acknowledge the fallen of other countries and to illustrate the differences in design and commemorative traditions. The book thus issues an invitation not only to Canadian readers but to those of all the countries affected by the Great War, to visit these sites of memory, so meaningful and moving, and to reflect upon the multi-faceted experiences and tragedies of one hundred years ago.

AFTER THE DIN OF BATTLE HE SLEEPS WELL IN PROUD MEMORY. FROM HIS WIFE.
Private Charles Maltby Molt, 14th Battalion, March 10th 1915 (age 27)

HE NEVER FALTERED.
Private Harry Pilcher-Clayton, 10th Battalion, May 21st 1915 (age 22)

HE HELPED AND DIED AND HIS DEATH WAS WORTHY OF THE MAN. R.I.P.
Private George Cain Bellamy, 15th Battalion, May 21st 1915 (age 20)

DEO DANTE DEDI.
[AS GOD GAVE, I GAVE.]
Lieutenant William Galbraith Tennant, Lord Strathcona's Horse, May 25th 1915 (age 36)

WE WHO KNEW THE SPLENDOUR OF HIS SOUL WILL NOT FORGET.
Sergeant LeRoy Launcelot Seeley, 3rd Battalion, May 25th 1915 (age 26)

HE PLAYED THE GAME.
Corporal William Frederic Longley Pilkington, 7th Battalion, May 25th 1915 (age 25)

BORN INVERNESS, APRIL 11TH 1883. DIED 1915 AFTER BATTLE OF FESTUBERT.
Lieutenant David Mundell, 5th Battalion, May 26th 1915 (age 32)

HE DIED FOR CANADA AND THE EMPIRE.
Private Robert Blake Allan, 16th Battalion, May 31st 1915 (age 20)

I COUNT MY LIFE WELL LOST TO SERVE MY COUNTRY BEST.
Captain George John Lorne Smith, 1st Battalion, June 15th 1915 (age 32)

AND THEY RISE TO THEIR FEET AS HE PASSES BY, GENTLEMEN UNFRAID.
Lieutenant Charles Loaring Clark, 3rd Battalion, June 17th 1915 (age 21)
[Rudyard Kipling, *Barrack-Room Ballads*]

HE GAVE HIS LIFE BRAVELY THAT OTHERS MIGHT LIVE. MOTHER
Private Thomas Albert Morgan, 13th Battalion, July 5th 1915 (age 16)

HE HATH RAISED HIM UP AND SET HIM WITH PRINCES. ENJOY THY RICH REWARD.
Private William John Cheese, 19th Battalion, September 17th 1915 (age 17)
[cf. Psalm 13:8]

WATCH AND PRAY, FOR YE KNOW NOT WHEN THE TIME IS.
Sapper John Bert Lang, Canadian Engineers, September 23rd 1915 (age 19)
[Mark 13:33]

IN EVER LOVING MEMORY OF A CHRISTIAN HERO AND A DEVOTED SON.
Private Leslie Ernest Unthank, 18th Battalion, October 13th 1915 (age 28)

NO THOUGHT OF SELF OR EARTHLY WEALTH BUT GAVE ALL FOR HOME AND LIBERTY.
Private Frederick Charles Whitcutt, 31st Battalion, November 15th 1915 (age 35)

HIS VIRTUES ARE RECORDED ELSEWHERE.
Sergeant George Henry Evans, 10th Battalion, November 20th 1915 (age 25)

HE SHALL BE MINE, SAITH THE LORD, THAT DAY WHEN I GATHER MY JEWELS.
Private Reginald Francis Trevor, 21st Battalion, November 27th 1915 (age 19)
[Cf. Malachi 3:17]

Etaples Military Cemetery

THE FIGHT THAT YE SO WELL BEGUN IS FINISHED NOW AND NOBLY WON.
Private Cecil Mumford, 3rd Canadian Mounted Rifles, December 1st 1915 (age 22)

HE GAVE HIS LIFE FOR THE WORLD, FOR YOU AND ME.
Private Harold Roy Flint, 3rd Battalion, December 30th 1915 (age 20)

I HEARD THE CALL AND ANSWERED IT.
Private James John Stokes, 49th Battalion, January 14th 1916 (age 25)

MORE LOYAL AND MORE LOVING HEART NEVER BEAT WITHIN HUMAN BREAST.
Private Frederick James Tupper, 3rd Battalion, March 9th 1916 (age 24)

OUR BABY BOY.
Private Lionel Wellington Nutter, 5th Canadian Mounted Rifles, March 25th 1916 (age 19)

A DIRECT DESCENDANT OF THE YOUNG CHIEF THAT FELL ON CULLODEN FIELD.
Private James Duncan Montgomery MacGillivray, 14th Battalion, April 25th 1916 (age 41)

OUR SON IS GONE. HE DID HIS BEST SO THE WORLD AT LARGE MAY REST.
Pioneer Edward Albert Birch, Canadian Pioneers, April 25th 1916 (age 34)

HE WAS DUTIFUL AND GAVE HIS LIFE FOR LIBERTY OF THE EMPIRE.
Private Joseph Craig, 2nd Battalion, April 26th 1916 (age 24)

I KNOW THAT TRUTH WAS YOURS AND ALL I LOVED YOU FOR OF OLD ENDURES.
Private William Manning, 16th Battalion, April 28th 1916 (age 26)

HERE LIES ONE OF MALTA'S GALLANT SONS.
Private Edgar Sapienza, 18th Battalion, April 26th 1916 (age 31)

YE ARE THE LIGHT OF THE WORLD. MATTHEW 5. 14.
Private Percy James Phillips, 7th Battalion, May 5th 1916 (age 26)

THY LIFE WAS GIVEN FOR ME. WHAT CAN I GIVE TO THEE, MY BROTHER?
Private Meiklejohn Wright, Canadian Army Medical Corps, May 11th 1916 (age 31)

Opposite: The Menin Gate at night.

IN ALL THY WORKS REMEMBER THY END AND THOU SHALT NEVER SIN. ECCL. 7. 40.
Lance Corporal James Frederick Lavelle, 1st Canadian Mounted Rifles, May 12th 1916 (age 27)

THAT LIFE IS LONG WHICH ANSWERS LIFE'S GREAT END.
Lieutenant George Henderson Campbell, Canadian Pioneers, May 16th 1916 (age 23)

MAY THE GREAT SOUL BE GREATER FOR MY SOUL. LAMPMAN
Lieutenant Thomas Harold Fennell, 2nd Canadian Mounted Rifles, May 17th 1916 (age 27)

HE DIED AT HIS POST. FATHER
Private Edward Pyne, 4th Battalion, May 26th 1916 (age 33)

THEY GAVE THEIR YOUNG LIVES THAT WE MAY LIVE.
Private George Hendry Young, 2nd Battalion, May 26th 1916 (age 27)

ALL GATES ARE GOOD THROUGH WHICH WE PASS TO GOD.
Private Edward Ford Abell, Canadian Army Service Corps, June 3rd 1916 (age 21)

HE SERVED.
Lance Corporal Archie Greene, Princess Patricia's Canadian Light Infantry, June 4th 1916 (age 27)

A LOVING SON, FOND BROTHER, TRUE FRIEND.
Lance Corporal Ivor Withers, 1st Canadian Mounted Rifles, June 5th 1916 (age 22)

FAITHFUL UNTO DEATH FOR THE CAUSE OF RIGHTEOUSNESS.
Private Alfred Gordon Travers, 5th Battalion, June 7th 1916 (age 32)

FOR PEACE.
Sergeant William Thomas Warwick, 1st Battalion, June 12th 1916 (age 40)

"MON ÂME À DIEU, MON COEUR À MA MÈRE, À MA PATRIE MON SANG ET MA VIE."
["MY SOUL TO GOD, MY HEART TO MY MOTHER, AND TO MY NATIVE LAND MY BLOOD AND MY LIFE."]
Private Omer Mallette, 22nd (French Canadian) Battalion, June 17th 1916 (age 23)

HE SAVED OTHERS, HIMSELF HE COULD NOT SAVE. IT'LL BE ENOUGH FOR NOW.
Sapper William Arthur Bower, Canadian Engineers, June 29th 1916 (age 22)

Opposite: Old trench lines running through Delville Wood, where South African soldiers fought on the Somme.

I GAVE MY ALL. I CAN DO NO MORE.
Pioneer John Conner, Canadian Pioneers, September 9th 1916 (age 35)

"THE JOURNEY IS DONE AND THE SUMMIT ATTAINED." BROWNING
Sergeant Arthur John Witchell, Canadian Engineers, September 12th 1916 (age 37)

THE FAREWELL ALWAYS LIES BEHIND US AND THE WELCOME ON BEFORE.
Private Robert Henry Killip, 2nd Canadian Mounted Rifles, September 12th 1916 (age 26)

FELL ON THE SOMME. ONLY SON OF C.B. WILSON M.D. FLORENCE & EDINBURGH.
Major Charles Blair Wilson, 42nd Battalion, September 15th 1916 (age 21)

BE THE DAY WEARY, BE THE DAY LONG, PRESENTLY RINGETH EVENSONG.
Private William Richard Frazier, Canadian Machine Gun Corps, September 15th 1916 (age 32)

A LA FLEUR DE L'AGE IL SACRIFIA HÉROÏQUEMENT SA VIE POUR SON PAYS.
[IN THE PRIME OF LIFE HE SACRIFICED HIS LIFE HEROICALLY FOR HIS COUNTRY.]
Captain Maurice Edouard Bauset, 22nd (French Canadian) Battalion, September 16th 1916 (age 27)

A LOVING SON, A TRUE PATRIOT.
Lieutenant Gordon Wilson Crow, Canadian Field Artillery, September 17th 1916 (age 23)

THERE IS NO GAIN EXCEPT BY LOSS. THERE IS NO LIFE EXCEPT BY DEATH.
Private Wendell Trueman Gray, Canadian Machine Gun Corps, September 17th 1916 (age 26)

HIS LIFE WAS BUT A VAPOUR. SOON IT VANISHED AWAY.
Private William Thomas Weeks, 5th Canadian Mounted Rifles, September 17th 1916 (age 23)

A GALLANT CANADIAN WHO GAVE HIS LIFE FOR HIS COUNTRY.
Lieutenant James Arlon Hamilton MC, 27th Battalion, September 18th 1916 (age 36)

ALL THROUGH LIFE I SEE TWO CROSSES.
Private James Gordon Small, Royal Canadian Regiment, September 18th 1916 (age 21)

THE MOVING FINGER WRITES, "HE LOVED HIS FELLOW MEN."
Private Richard Cavill, 20th Battalion, September 18th 1916 (age 28)

Opposite: A winter morning at Tyne Cot Cemetery.

LORD, IF THOU HADST BEEN THERE, MY BROTHER HAD NOT DIED. JOHN XI. 21
Private Henry Einar Dixon, 3rd Battalion, September 19th 1916 (age 29)

MAY THY SACRIFICE BRING TO THEE PEACE AND CONTENT ETERNALLY.
Lieutenant Conrad George Carey, 43rd Battalion, September 21st 1916 (age 23)

A HERO. WRITE UPON HIS GRAVE, HE DIED THAT BRITAIN MIGHT ENDURE.
Private William Douglas Heatley, 43rd Battalion, September 23rd 1916 (age 23)

WHILE THE LIGHT LASTS WE SHALL REMEMBER AND IN THE DARKNESS NOT FORGET.
Private George Frederick Swallow, 15th Battalion, September 26th 1916 (age 30)

GOD NEVER IMPOSES A DUTY WITHOUT GIVING THE TIME TO DO IT.
DEEPLY MOURNED. WIFE & DAUGHTER
Private Robert Frier Cunningham, 5th Battalion, September 26th 1916 (age 26)

THOUGH ONLY A BOY HE PLAYED A MAN'S PART. A HERO BELOVED OF ALL.
Private Arthur John Allan, 10th Battalion, September 27th 1916 (age 25)

HE HESITATED NOT WHEN DUTY CALLED.
Private Joseph William Wharrie, 4th Canadian Mounted Rifles, September 29th 1916

HE DIED SO THAT LIFE MIGHT BE A SWEETER THING TO ALL. HE LIVETH.
Private William Sime, 28th Battalion, September 29th 1916 (age 37)

DEO LEGI REGI GREGI.
[FOR GOD, THE LAW, THE KING, AND THE PEOPLE.]
Gunner Karl Blair McCormick, Canadian Field Artillery, September 30th 1916 (age 21)

THOSE THOU KEEPEST ALWAYS SEE LIGHT AT EVENTIDE. FROM WIFE & SONS
Private Charles Trigg, 2nd Canadian Mounted Rifles, September 30th 1916 (age 39)

VIVE LE CANADA. L.L. BELL, GRAND SAULT, N.B. EST MORT POUR L'EUROPE.
[LONG LIVE CANADA. L.L. BELL, GRAND SAULT, N.B., DIED FOR EUROPE.]
Corporal Louis Leo Bell, 26th Battalion, October 4th 1916 (age 28)

The German war cemetery at Neuville-St. Vaast, near Vimy Ridge, has nearly 45,000 graves. Note the tablet in the upper left corner – it marks the place of one of the 12,000 German Jews who fell for their country in the First World War.

THOSE WHO LIVED AND THOSE WHO DIED, THEY WERE ONE IN NOBLE PRIDE.
Private William Patrick Ryan, 13th Battalion, October 8th 1916 (age 31)

YOUNG, STRONG, FREE, HE DIED THAT WE MIGHT LIVE. GREATER LOVE HATH NO MAN.
Private Edgar Walker Priestley, 49th Battalion, October 8th 1916 (age 20)

WHAT TIME I AM AFRAID I WILL TRUST IN THEE. PSALMS LVI.3
Private John Alfred Moffit, 13th Battalion, October 8th 1916 (age 20)

ONLY A BOY BUT HE DID HIS BEST. NOT FORGOTTEN.
Private Henry Childs, 13th Battalion, October 8th 1916 (age 20)

FAR FROM HIS CANADIAN HOME OUR SOLDIER BOY IS SLEEPING.
Lieutenant Elmer Clark Bryson, 13th Battalion, October 8th 1916 (age 23)

DEATH HAS MADE HIS DARKNESS MORE BEAUTIFUL WITH THEE.
Major Fred Rowan, 13th Battalion, October 9th 1916 (age 25)

A SON OF ENGLAND – FROM CANADA, GIVEN TO THE EMPIRE.
2nd Lieutenant Francis Matt Lawledge, Royal Engineers, October 10th 1916 (age 38)

SEEING DUTY FIRST HE WENT AT ONCE AS TO A SACRAMENT.
Private Harry Edward Bagsley, Princess Patricia's Canadian Light Infantry, October 10th 1916

I HAVE NOT FEARED WHAT MAN CAN DO FOR I ON GOD RELY.
Lieutenant Harry Austin McCleave, 13th Battalion, October 10th 1916 (age 24)

THE RIGHTEOUS SHALL BE IN EVERLASTING REMEMBRANCE. PSALM 112 6TH VERSE
Major Charles Donald Livingstone, 1st Canadian Mounted Rifles, October 12th 1916 (age 43)

HE SPRANG TO DUTY'S CALL AND PAID THE PRICE.
Private Charles Walker, 4th Canadian Mounted Rifles, October 12th 1916 (age 26)

FRANK! JESUS CALLS. WITH DUTY DONE FOR ALL, YOU WERE READY. FATHER
Private Frank Waltho, 75th Battalion, October 13th 1916 (age 20)

The Caribou Memorial at Beaumont-Hamel, Newfoundland Memorial Park, the Somme

WE ARE ONLY REMEMBERED BY WHAT WE HAVE DONE.
Private George Brookes Wilson, 2nd Battalion, October 13th 1916 (age 31)

ALLAN MY NAME, CANADA MY NATION, OTTAWA MY BIRTHPLACE, HEAVENLY EXPECTATION.
Private Allan John Burke, 38th Battalion, October 15th 1916 (age 32)

THE MEASURE OF LIFE IS NOT ITS SPAN BUT THE USE MADE OF IT.
Private William Pewtress, 87th Battalion, October 16th 1916 (age 26)

KILLED IN ACTION, BATTLE OF THE SOMME, FOR KING AND COUNTRY.
Pioneer Edward Cosmo Innes, Canadian Pioneers, October 22nd 1916 (age 22)

MORE BRAVE FOR THIS, THAT HE HAD MUCH TO LOVE.
Driver Andrew Donaldson, Canadian Field Artillery, November 2nd 1916 (age 21)

HE GAVE HIS LIFE THAT MORTALS MAY FIND HOPE BEYOND THEIR TEARS.
Gunner Austin Kyle, Canadian Field Artillery, November 10th 1916 (age 22)

HE VOLUNTEERED. HE THOUGHT IT WAS HIS DUTY. HE DIED THAT WE MAY LIVE.
Private John Thomas Jardine, 8th Battalion, November 11th 1916 (age 20)

DANSK FRIVILLIG BEVARET I KAERLIG ERINDRING AF SINE KAERE I DANMARK.
[A DANISH VOLUNTEER KEPT IN LOVING MEMORY BY HIS LOVED ONES IN DENMARK.]
Private Victor Hugo Sørensen, 4th Battalion, November 12th 1916 (age 31)

SAFETY WHERE NO FOE APPROACHES, PEACE WHERE STRIFE SHALL BE O'ER.
Private Norman Willard McLaren, 73rd Battalion, November 13th 1916 (age 20)

THE WORLD GAINED BY HIS SACRIFICE.
Sergeant Lewis Robertson, Canadian Machine Gun Corps, November 22nd 1916 (age 22)

FOR LOVE, THE SERVICE OF OUR LIVES TO KEEP FREE THE LAND HE SERVED.
Sapper Lloyd Brubacher, Canadian Engineers, November 25th 1916 (age 22)

"HE SHALL HAVE DOMINION FROM SEA TO SEA." PS. LXXII. 8
Major Sydney Lodge Thorne, 60th Battalion, November 26th 1916 (age 37)

Opposite: Brothers killed at Passchendaele and buried side by side in Tyne Cot Cemetery.

MY SON, MY SON.
Private George Thorn, 58th Battalion, December 12th 1916 (age 32)

HE IS SACRED, HIGH IN OUR MEMORY, AND TO GOD WE CAN LEAVE THE REST.
Private Samuel Ramsden, 72nd Battalion, December 27th 1916 (age 18)

HE SHALL GATHER TOGETHER HIS ELECT FROM THE FOUR WINDS.
Corporal John William McInnes, Princess Patricia's Canadian Light Infantry, January 4th 1917 (age 26)
[Mark 13:27]

SAFE FROM THE WORLD'S TEMPTATIONS.
Private Archibald Hugh Linton, 46th Battalion, January 16th 1917 (age 20)

GOD GRANT, THAT HE MAY BE A MESSENGER OF LOVE BETWEEN US.
Private William James Grist, 20th Battalion, January 17th 1917 (age 29)

A LANCASHIRE LAD WHO HEARD HIS COUNTRY'S CALL.
Private William Adam Dent, 21st Battalion, January 17th 1917 (age 32)

LOVED, YET STEADFAST, SET TO DO HIS PART.
Private Percy James Hodge, 20th Battalion, January 17th 1917 (age 21)

NONE OF US LIVETH TO HIMSELF AND NO MAN DIETH TO HIMSELF.
Private Frank Honeywell Magee, 7th Battalion, January 24th 1917 (age 22)
[Romans 14:7]

MEDICAL STAFF. DIED OF WOUNDS. UNDYING LOVE, MOTHER & WIFE
Private Henry Gardner, 38th Battalion, February 22nd 1917 (age 20)

BORN JUNE 23RD 1897. HE LOVED RIGHT MORE THAN PEACE.
Gunner Thomas Vernal Waldon, Canadian Field Artillery, February 22nd 1917 (age 19)

GWELL ANGEU NA CHYWILYDD.
[BETTER DEATH THAN SHAME.]
Private Robert Evan Jones, 46th Battalion, February 26th 1917 (age 23)

Maurice Cullen *Dawn on the Ouse Trench*
[CWM 19710261-0130 Beaverbrook Collection of War Art, Canadian War Museum]

HIS BEAUTIFUL LIFE AND CHARACTER WERE AN INSPIRATION
TO ALL HIS COMRADES. (MOTHER)
Private Arthur Frederick Cordy, 1st Battalion, February 27th 1917 (age 23)

OF THE ROMAN CATHOLIC FAITH AND VIRTUOUS. DIED FOR KING AND COUNTRY. R.I.P.
Private Stephen David Johnston, 73rd Battalion, March 1st 1917 (age 26)

I SHALL ARRIVE, WHAT TIME, WHAT CIRCUIT FIRST I ASK NOT.
Major James Miles Langstaff, 75th Battalion, March 1st 1917 (age 33)
[Robert Browning, "Paracelsus"]

TWAS MY CHEERFUL DUTY.
Private James Ingham, 73rd Battalion, March 1st 1917 (age 18)

BY HIS DEATH OUR LIFE REVEALING, HE FOR US THE RANSOM PAID.
Private Alexander Robert Dunn, 78th Battalion, March 1st 1917 (age 33)

FOR THE GLORY OF THE GRAND OLD FLAG.
Company Sergeant Major Angus Stewart Donald, 75th Battalion, March 2nd 1917 (age 32)

THE DEATH HE DIED TO SAVE US, VICTOR IN THAT AWFUL STRIFE.
Lieutenant Joseph Griffiths MC, 73rd Battalion, March 2nd 1917

MY ONLY SON, CHUM AND COMPANION FOR 28 YEARS. HIS SISTER AND I MISS HIM.
Private William MacLean Kennedy, Canadian Army Medical Corps, March 8th 1917 (age 29)

SCARCE BOY, YET MAN, WITH TORCH HELD HIGH, HIS SCROLL FOR US TO DIE.
Private Francis Reuben Brown, 102nd Battalion, March 23rd 1917 (age 18)

FOR FREEDOM HE GAVE HIS LAST FULL MEASURE OF DEVOTION. MOTHER
Private Oliver Mowat Hogg, Princess Patricia's Canadian Light Infantry, March 24th 1917 (age 25)

POUR SA PATRIE ET LA FRANCE IL A SACRIFIÉ SA VIE. PARENTS ALSATIENS
[HE SACRIFICED HIS LIFE FOR HIS COUNTRY AND FOR FRANCE. ALSATIAN PARENTS]
Driver Charles Ernest Wehrle, Canadian Army Service Corps, March 24th 1917 (age 23)

Bedford House Cemetery

HERE LIES MY LOVING SON TO REST IN SILENCE.
WE WEEP FOR OUR LOVED ONE LEFT BEHIND.
Private Harry William Wyman, 75th Battalion, March 30th 1917 (age 18)

ONE CROWDED HOUR OF GLORIOUS LIFE IS WORTH AN AGE WITHOUT NAME.
Lieutenant William Robert Boucher, 46th Battalion, March 26th 1917 (age 24)

HE FOLLOWED WITH THE BRAVE AND BEST IN GOD'S GREAT ADVANCE.
Private Robert Lawson, 46th Battalion, March 30th 1917 (age 36)

HIS AMBITION WAS NO HONOURS, ONLY A CLEAN SHEET.
Private Clarence Gibson, 73rd Battalion, April 4th 1917 (age 21)

I GAVE MY ALL FOR GOD, KING AND COUNTRY. MOTHER
Private William Hebdon, 2nd Battalion, April 4th 1917 (age 21)

ONE I LOVED BEST WAS AMONG THE REST WHO DIED, MOTHERLAND, FOR YOU. BILLIE
Private George Henry Gaskin, 5th Battalion, April 5th 1917 (age 36)

ONLY A BOY PLAYING A MAN'S PART, GIVING HIS LIFE FOR FREEDOM'S CAUSE.
Private Douglass Clark, 1st Battalion, April 5th 1917 (age 17)

"HE SAW THE SPIRIT OF GOD DESCENDING LIKE A DOVE." MATTHEW 3: 16
Private John Laidlaw, 1st Canadian Mounted Rifles, April 7th/10th 1917 (age 22)

QUI ANTE DIEM PERIIT, SED MILES, SED PRO PATRIA.
[HE DIED BEFORE HIS TIME, BUT AS A SOLDIER, FOR HIS COUNTRY.]
Lieutenant Colonel Woodman Leonard DSO, Canadian Field Artillery, April 9th 1917 (age 34)

VIVIT POST FUNERA VIRTUS.
[VIRTUE LIVES ON AFTER DEATH.]
Sergeant Mervyn Mansell Lupton, 7th Battalion, April 9th 1917 (age 23)

"THESE BE THE GLORIOUS ENDS WHERETO WE PASS." KIPLING
Private Michael Alfred Stanton, Canadian Machine Gun Corps, April 9th 1917 (age 19)

Opposite: Names of the missing on the Vimy Memorial.

PRIVATES J.BEAD W.H.EADES C.EADIE W.O.EAGLE A.R.EAGLES C.H.EAGLESTONE H.A.EARL W.EARLE G.EARLS J.EA
ELDRIDGE W.K.ELDRIDGE G.ELEMENT H.ELEY E.R.ELFORD E.G.ELKINS R.W.ELKINS SERVED AS R.CHOULES W.S.E
ERICKSON C.ERRINGTON H.D.ERVIN G.I.ESPELAND G.ESSELMONT T.A.ESSERY T.SESSON T.ETCHELLS C.ETHER
FOLKARD R.FOUBISTER H.FOWLER J.W.FRASER LANCE CORPORALS R.N.FAIR A.G.FANCOURT E.FARLEY J.F
FARROW S.B.FARROW W.T.FARROW F.S.FAUCHON J.FAULDER F.F.FAULKE C.T.FAULKNER A.FAURE M.M. R.J.FAVEL J.F
D.FINLAYSON SERVED AS D.DOUGLAS N.FINLEY J.L.FINNERAN T.J.FINNESSEY G.T.FINNNETT F.FINNIE W.FINNIE W.F
FOLEY M.FOLEY W.FOLEY G.FOLLETT A.FONTAINE R.FONTAINE F.FOOTE R.G.FOOTE D.FOOTURANSKY A.McI.FORE
FRANCE A.E.FRANCIS D.FRANCIS H.W.FRANCIS P.E.FRANCIS W.J.FRANCIS J.FRANKLIN J.M.FRANKLIN A.FRASER C.FRAS
ILKER L.S.GYSIN CAPTAIN A.S.GODDARD LIEUTENANTS R.L.GEDDES E.V.GELL J.A.GERVAIS A.P.GIBAUT H.
GALE G.N.GALLINGER T.R.GAMMAN L.GAUGHAN A.GAVINE G.H.GIBSON R.M.GIBSON J.P.GILLIS O.GILLIS
ALBRAITH A.T.GALE J.T.GALE J.A.GALLAGHER J.P.GALLAGHER T.J.GALLAGHER W.M.GALLAGHER I.GALLA
ASKELL A.GATES F.R.GATES J.GATES J.A.GATES C.GATTI W.F.GATWARD V.A.GAUDET P.GAUDETTE R.C.
IBSON W.A.GIEBNER T.A.GIFFEN R.GIGANT R.R.GIGNAC J.O.GILBERT R.GILBERT S.GILBEY G.GILCHREST
ODWIN G.A.GODWIN R.GODWIN W.W.GOHEEN M.M. H.V.GOLDEN M.M. W.J.GOLDEN A.GOLDIE L.E.GOLDING
TELL J.GOUDREAU A.GOUEDARD B.GOUGH F.E.GOUGH H.GOUGH J.GOUGH E.A.GOULD N.GOULD W.C
EAVES S.GREAYER A.GREEN A.A.GREEN A.E.GREEN A.H.GREEN A.J.GREEN A.T.GREEN 412116 A.W.GREEN
RIESBACH A.GRIFFIN C.F.GRIFFIN C.H.GRIFFIN J.GRIFFIN L.A.GRIFFIN R.N.GRIFFIN V.E.GRIFFIN F.L.GRIFFIS
MAJOR H.HUTCHINS CAPTAINS J.G.HELLIWELL E.H.HOLLAND MC H.J.HORAN LIEUTENANTS C.HADD
HALLET R.G.HILL E.HITT G.HULME CORPORALS J.J.HANCOX W.S.HANNAY W.J.HARE T.HARRIS C.A
LMWOOD R.A.HOOD S.C.HOOD E.C.HOSKINS A.W.HOUSE E.H.P.HOWARD R.R.HOWDEN A.W.HOWE J.HOW
GGETT M.HAGLE A.HAGUE C.L.HAIGHT E.W.HAIGHT W.H.HAIGHT G.HAINES G.A.R.HAINES F.HAIRE R.HA
MILTON J.W.F.HAMILTON McG.HAMILTON R.HAMILTON SERVED AS R.KANE R.L.HAMILTON T.HAMILTON V
MAN C.HARDY F.L.HARDY J.T.HARDY F.HARGREAVES W.HARGREAVES G.O.HARKIN J.HARKNESS D.HA
TLEY W.H.HARTLEY A.G.HARTT J.T.H.HARTT A.E.HARVEY A.O.HARVEY D.W.HARVEY H.HARVEY H.W.H
YES W.E.HAYES W.J.HAYES S.HAYMAN B.HAYNES F.T.HAYNES J.HAYNES W.H.HAYNES R.HAYS E.T.HAYTE
NDERSON G.W.HENDERSON 152440 H.HENDERSON 453818 H.HENDERSON 13510 J.HENDERSON 163836 J.HEN
VITT P.D.HEWITT R.HEWITT J.E.HEYES H.HICK H.G.HICKEY S.HICKEY H.S.HICKLING T.HICKLING C.F.H
IN W.H.HODGIN L.E.HODGINS S.E.HODGINS W.J.HODGINS A.HODGSON G.M.HODGSON H.R.HODGSON
LMES C.B.HOLT J.HOLT W.H.HOLT D.H.HOLTUM T.HOMES W.HOMEWOOD C.D.HONE D.F.HONEY G.F.HONEY
HOWELL L.HOWELLS S.J.HOWES M.HOWIE G.HOWLES A.F.HOWLETT H.T.HOWLETT W.HOWLETT C.E.HUBBA
A.G.HUNTLEY F.G.HUNWICK C.L.HURD C.W.HURLEY J.G.HURLEY W.G.HURLEY J.G.HURRY C.G.A.HURST C.I
E.A.INNES G.INNES T.INNES W.INNES T.G.IREDALE H.IRELAND J.IRELAND T.IRELAND T.W.IRELAND F.E.IP
J.A.JOHNSTON T.J.JOHNSTON W.C.JOHNSTON G.B.JOHNSTONE G.JONES P.E.JONES R.H.JONES W.JONES W.J
A.JASKALA D.P.JAY A.JEANS G.JEANS A.L.JEAVONS F.JEBBETT A.JEFFERIES F.J.JEFFERSON W.JEFFERS
12306 W.JOHNSON 141702 W.JOHNSON 811671 W.JOHNSON 2448444 W.JOHNSON W.C.JO
E.A.JONES E.J.JONES E.K.JONES 252303 F.JONES 707102 F.JONES G.G.T.JONES 105347 H
J.M.KELSON J.H.KENNEDY R.W.KERR R.KEY G.KING A.KNIGHT H.
L.KAVANAGH T.J.KEARNEY T.KEATING W.E.KEATING C

The Cross of Sacrifice at Tyne Cot Cemetery was built over a German bunker. Nearby are four German graves included by the architects in a gesture of reconciliation.

THE LORD OF PEACE HIMSELF GIVE YOU PEACE ALWAYS. 2 THESS. III.16
Lieutenant Frank Fernie McGowen, 16th Battalion, April 9th 1917 (age 36)

AT PEACE WITH GOD. YOU SMILE BACK AND NEVER KNOW REGRET.
Lieutenant Reginald Lawrence Sladen, Princess Patricia's Canadian Light Infantry, April 9th 1917 (age 19)

SUCH IS THE WAY TO IMMORTALITY.
Private Willie Pyke, 5th Battalion, April 9th 1917 (age 20)

FROM THE FIELD OF BATTLE TO THE PEACE OF GOD.
Private John Town, 5th Battalion, April 9th 1917 (age 26)

A MAN.
Corporal John James Burke, Royal Canadian Regiment, April 9th 1917 (age 29)

SO SOON PASSETH IT AWAY AND WE ARE GONE. PS. 90.10
Private Harold George Carter, 73rd Battalion, April 20th 1917 (age 21)

WE BOW IN DEEP SUBMISSION TO OUR HEAVENLY FATHER'S WILL.
Private Stephen Peyton, Royal Newfoundland Regiment, April 28th 1917 (age 23)

OUR BOY, ENGLAND'S MAN.
Private Henry Griffin, 16th Battalion, April 28th 1917 (age 21)

THE LORD SHALL GIVE HIS PEOPLE THE BLESSING OF PEACE.
Private John McCallum LeRoy, 5th Battalion, April 28th 1917 (age 30)
[Psalm 29:11]

HE, BEING PERFECTED, IN A SHORT TIME FULFILLED LONG DAYS.
Lieutenant Joseph Plimsoll Edwards, Canadian Engineers, April 28th 1917 (age 25)
[Wisdom of Solomon 4:13]

TO ALL THOSE WHOSE NOBLE FEALTY GAVE LIFE ITSELF TO SET LIFE FREE, THY PRAISE.
Lieutenant William Kitchener Kift, 116th Battalion, April 29th 1917 (age 17)

OF HIS OWN FREE WILL AND ACCORD.
Private James Bradford Davidson, 10th Battalion, May 1st 1917 (age 19)

"FLOODS CANNOT QUENCH THE LOVE OF A PARENT." GOD IS LOVE.
Driver Leonard William Warren, Canadian Army Medical Corps, May 2nd 1917

HE DIED THAT WE MIGHT LIVE AND LOVE AND SERVE.
Private Walter Joab Martin, 1st Battalion, May 3rd 1917 (age 21)

REMEMBERING YOU WE WILL BE BRAVE & STRONG.
Sergeant William Beattie, 31st Battalion, May 3rd 1917 (age 25)

BORN ON SHIP "STANLEY" ON INDIAN OCEAN, 23RD JUNE 1894. MY BELOVED SON.
Lieutenant Louis Stanley Edgett, 60th Battalion, May 10th 1917 (age 22)

TIME BUT THE IMPRESSION DEEPER MAKES.
Lance Corporal Andrew Ramage, Princess Patricia's Canadian Light Infantry, May 17th 1917 (age 28)
[Robert Burns, "To Mary in Heaven"]

FORTH FROM THE SHADOWS CAME DEATH WITH THE PITILESS SYLLABLE "NOW."
Major Anthony Lavelle McHugh, Canadian Railway Troops, May 19th 1917 (age 53)

HIS DEATH IS A WOUND UNTIL DEATH TO THOSE WHO LOVED HIM.
Private Arthur Gamble, 44th Battalion, June 3rd 1917 (age 31)

OUR DEARLY LOVED AND ONLY CHILD TEDDY.
Lieutenant George Edward Ambery, 50th Battalion, June 3rd 1917 (age 23)

DORS EN PAIX, BOBI, SOUS LE SOL DE TES PÈRES.
[REST IN PEACE, BOBBY, BENEATH THE SOIL OF YOUR FATHERS.]
Private Robert Joseph Georges, 102nd Battalion, June 8th 1917 (age 21)

HE VOLUNTARILY GAVE HIS LIFE FOR FREEDOM.
Corporal Robert Alexander Muir, 85th Battalion, June 19th 1917 (age 26)

IS IT NOTHING TO YOU ALL YE THAT PASS BY? LAMENTATIONS 1.12.
Private Arthur Smith, 5th Battalion, June 28th 1917 (age 26)

Opposite: The restored trenches at Vimy Ridge outlined in the snow.

THE SACRIFICE HE MADE IS SURELY AN OFFERING ACCEPTABLE TO OUR LORD.
Private William Henry Taberner, 58th Battalion, June 28th 1917 (age 20)

AN INDIAN. TO HIS COUNTRY'S CALL DOING HIS DUTY. THAT IS ALL.
Private William Turner, 52nd Battalion, July 6th 1917 (age 35)

MY COUNTRY BEFORE EVEN YOU, MOTHER DEAR
(HIS PARTING WORDS ON LEAVING HOME).
Lieutenant John Clarence Hanson, 104th Battalion, July 17th 1917 (age 24)

AU ROI ET À LA PATRIE UN FILS DU CANADA A NOBLEMENT TOUT DONNÉ.
[TO KING AND COUNTRY A SON OF CANADA HAS NOBLY GIVEN ALL.]
Private Joseph Charland, 22nd (French Canadian) Battalion, July 17th 1917 (age 22)

"THE UNDONE YEARS, THE CRUELTY OF WAR."
SADLY MISSED BY MOTHER, FATHER, SISTERS, BROS.
Private Charles Albert Rollings, 52nd Battalion, July 18th 1917 (age 26)

LORD, WE LOVED HIM. HAD GOD ASKED US, WELL WE KNOW,
WE WOULD CRY, O SPARE THIS BLOW.
Private Edward Fagan, 14th Battalion, August 8th 1917 (age 23)

SHARP HAS YOUR FROST OF WINTER BEEN BUT BRIGHT SHALL BE YOUR SPRING.
Private George Murphy, 8th Battalion, August 15th 1917 (age 30)

THERE IS SOMETHING SUBLIME IN CALM ENDURANCE.
Lance Corporal Ralph Osborne Kempton, 87th Battalion, August 15th 1917 (age 25)

A MAN IN A WORLD OF MEN. LOVED BY ALL.
Pioneer Albert Normington, Canadian Pioneers, August 15th 1917 (age 33)

HE LOVED CHIVALRY, TRUTH AND HONOUR, FREEDOM AND COURTESY.
Private Oliver Bilton, 24th Battalion, August 15th 1917 (age 27)

ADIEU, PARENTS, JE MEURS POUR DIEU, LE ROI ET MA PATRIE.
[FAREWELL, PARENTS, I DIE FOR GOD, THE KING AND MY COUNTRY.]
Private Eugène Bariel, 22nd (French Canadian) Battalion, August 15th 1917 (age 22)

French cemeteries, such as La Targette near Neuville-St. Vaast reveal, more powerfully than can any words, the impact of the Great War on France.

ÞINN FAÐIR HÆST Á HIMNUM ER, HANS HJARTA BIÐUR EFTIR ÞÉR.
[YOUR FATHER IS HIGHEST IN HEAVEN; HIS HEART AWAITS YOU.]
Private John Gilbert Johnson, 10th Battalion, August 15th 1917 (age 18)

HE FOUGHT THE FOES OF CANADA AND DIED ON A BATTLE-FIELD.
Private William Henry Hill, 8th Battalion, August 15th 1917 (age 34)

I LIFT MY CROSS EACH DAY AND THINK OF THEE, BRAVE HEART. HOME FOLKS
Lieutenant William Henry Clipperton, 8th Battalion, August 17th 1917 (age 31)

HE DIED THAT OTHERS MIGHT LIVE. HE WROUGHT HIS COUNTRY LASTING GOOD.
Private Charles Auguste Mougenel, 15th Battalion, August 22nd 1917 (age 43)

UNTO THE UPRIGHT ARISETH LIGHT IN THE DARKNESS. PSA. 112. 4.
Private Clayton George Whitman, 52nd Battalion, August 24th 1917 (age 20)

STILL ACHIEVING, STILL PURSUING, LEARN TO LABOUR AND TO WAIT.
Sergeant James Crawford Hunter, 54th Battalion, August 24th 1917 (age 38)
[Henry Wadsworth Longfellow, "A Psalm of Life"]

AM ARTHUR WIR MAE HIRAETH IN FAWR ER YR AWR YR AETH. EI DAD EI FAM
[WE HAVE LONGED FOR ARTHUR SINCE THE TIME HE LEFT US. HIS FATHER AND MOTHER]
Private Arthur Jones, Canadian Machine Gun Corps, September 14th 1917 (age 28)

HE WOULD GIVE HIS DINNER TO A HUNGRY DOG AND GO WITHOUT HIMSELF.
Gunner Charles Douglas Moore, Canadian Anti-Aircraft Battery, September 19th 1917 (age 30)

SAFE IN THE ARMS OF JESUS, BUT O, HOW I MISS YOU, DEAR. MOTHER
Private William Young, 5th Canadian Mounted Rifles, October 30th 1917 (age 19)

SAY WHAT A SOLDIER, A BROTHER, YEA A SON SHOULD BE, HE WAS THAT.
Private Foster Cecil Pawsey, 5th Battalion, November 26th 1917 (age 24)

ONE OF AMERICAN HARVARD VANGUARD, ENTERING CANADIAN SERVICE IN 1916.
Lieutenant Phillip Comfort Starr, Royal Engineers, February 20th 1918 (age 28)

Wimereux Communal Cemetery, where Lieutenant-Colonel John McCrae lies buried, contains 2,853 burials.
The high winds and sandy soil along the coast here made it necessary to lay the headstones flat.

Thurstan Topham *Opening of the Somme Bombardment*
[CWM 19710261-0728 Beaverbrook Collection of War Art, Canadian War Museum]

HE DIED TO HELP THE MAPLE LEAF TO LIVE.
Private Richard Russell Reeve, 16th Battalion, March 4th 1918 (age 23)

GRANDVIEW, MAN. BRAVE BUGLER BOY.
Lance Corporal Frederick Charles Davies, Canadian Pioneers, March 4th 1918 (age 19)

A GOOD MAN, A DEVOTED SON, A PROMPT VOLUNTEER.
Private Leonard Baker, 5th Battalion, March 13th 1918 (age 26)

A GENERAL FAVORITE, HONORED & LOVED BY SCHOOL CHUMS & FRIENDS.
Private Josh Cook, 38th Battalion, March 27th 1918 (age 22)

I WILL GO WITHOUT A MURMUR AND HIS FOOTSTEPS FOLLOW STILL.
Gunner Oscar George Plewis, Canadian Field Artillery, March 31st 1918 (age 22)

AT REST. EASTER SUNDAY.
Sergeant William Ernest Clark, Canadian Field Artillery, March 31st 1918 (age 35)

HVI BERST SVO BURT I SKYNDI HIN BESTA LIEFSINS GJOF.
[WHY IS LIFE'S BEST GIFT SO SUDDENLY TAKEN AWAY FROM US.]
Private Thorvaldur Thorvaldson, 16th Battalion, April 16th 1918 (age 21)

THERE'S NOT AN HOUR OF DAY OR DREAMING NIGHT BUT I AM WITH THEE.
Bombardier John Turnbull Wood, Canadian Field Artillery, April 5th 1918 (age 30)

HE DIED THAT OTHER VALIANT SOULS HE LOVED SHOULD LIVE TO FIGHT.
Lieutenant John Alexander Gouick, Canadian Field Artillery, April 15th 1918 (age 26)

WHILE THE RACES OF MANKIND ENDURE LET HIS EXAMPLE STAND.
Major Alan Torrance Powell DSO, 14th Battalion, April 19th 1918 (age 31)

LIKE CHRIST HE THOUGHT OF OTHERS.
Private Alexander Armstrong, 19th Battalion, April 26th 1918 (age 33)

HIS BETTER DOES NOT BREATHE UPON THIS EARTH.
Private Alfred William Manning, 27th Battalion, April 27th 1918 (age 28)

MAJOR 156TH BN. BROCKVILLE, ONT. PERFECT SOLDIER, GOOD SON, TRUE FRIEND.
Captain Herbert Hamilton Edwards, 21st Battalion, May 11th 1918 (age 36)

THE NOBLE ARMY OF MARTYRS PRAISE THEE.
Nursing Sister Gladys Maude Mary Wake, Canadian Army Nursing Service, May 21st 1918 (age 34)

NÉ LE 25 NOVEMBRE 1893. DÉCÉDÉ SUITE D'ÉCLAT D'OBUS.
[BORN 25 NOVEMBER 1893. DIED FOLLOWING A SHELLBURST.]
Private Hubert Debons, 22nd (French Canadian) Battalion, May 28th 1918 (age 24)

SHE DID HER DUTY FOR KING AND COUNTRY.
Nursing Sister Margaret Lowe, Canadian Army Nursing Service, May 28th 1918 (age 32)

CHAILL MI CUIDEACHADH MNAIR A CHAILL MI THU. I LOST MY HELP WHEN I LOST YOU.
Private Allan McIntyre MM and Bar, 25th Battalion, June 5th 1918 (age 25)

MORT GLORIEUSEMENT AU CHAMP D'HONNEUR À NEUVILLE-VITASSE, ARRAS.
[DIED GLORIOUSLY ON THE FIELD OF HONOUR AT NEUVILLE-VITASSE, ARRAS.]
Corporal Joseph Kaeble VC, 22nd (French Canadian) Battalion, June 9th 1918 (age 25)

BRITISH COLUMBIA INDIAN. DIED FOR KING AND COUNTRY.
Private Noel Seymour, Canadian Forestry Corps, June 10th 1918 (age 33)

BORN IN SPENCER, MASS., U.S.A. 1885. WOUNDED THREE TIMES, KILLED IN ACTION.
Private George Girouard, 22nd (French Canadian) Battalion, June 18th 1918 (age 34)

FOR I THE LORD THY GOD WILL HOLD THY RIGHT HAND. ISA. 41. 13
Sergeant George Hiram Clark, 8th Battalion, July 24th 1918 (age 31)

A HERO OF THREE WARS. GONE BUT NOT FORGOTTEN.
Sapper Alfred James, Canadian Railway Troops, August 1st 1918 (age 41)

GREAT PEACE HAVE THEY WHICH LOVE THY LAW.
Lieutenant Colonel Bartlett McLennan DSO, 42nd Battalion, August 3rd 1918 (age 49)
[Psalm 119:165]

HE TOOK MY PLACE. FATHER
Lieutenant Edward Fox Thairs, 3rd Battalion, August 8th 1918 (age 23)

A JOLLIE GOODE BOOKE WHEREON TO LOOKE WAS BETTER TO ME THAN GOLD.
Corporal Hugh Milroy Gilchrist, Canadian Machine Gun Corps, August 8th 1918 (age 26)

The headstone of Pioneer Dominick Naplava, a Czech volunteer who enlisted with the Canadian Expeditionary Force and was killed at Passchendaele. His is the only Commonwealth headstone from the First World War with an epitaph in Czech (although there are several examples of Czech inscriptions on Canadian graves from the Second World War). When the headstone was replaced in 2014, the original was donated to a museum in Prague. The epitaph is translated on page 138.

WE ARE THINKING OF YOU EVERY MINUTE. FATHER, MOTHER, SISTERS, BROTHERS
Sergeant Alexander Urquhart McLeod MM, Canadian Engineers, August 9th 1918 (25)

HEAVEN GIVES ITS FAVORITES EARLY DEATH.
Private Victor Cecil Potts, 2nd Canadian Mounted Rifles, August 10th 1918 (age 20)

DISCHARGED FROM N.Z. FORCES AS UNFIT, HAVING LOST THE SIGHT OF AN EYE.
RE-ENLISTED AT VANCOUVER.
Private Arthur Norman Hackney, 29th Battalion, August 9th 1918 (age 36)

LOVE AND REMEMBRANCE TWINE ROUND HIS NAME.
Private Robert Henry Smith Horwood, 43rd Battalion, August 16th 1918 (age 20)

GOD GRANT WE MAY BE WORTHY OF ALL THESE SPLENDID LIVES.
Major Frederick Leopold Hesson, 78th Battalion, August 24th 1918 (age 31)

DITES LEUR QUE J'AI FAIT MON DEVOIR.
[TELL THEM THAT I DID MY DUTY.]
Lieutenant Louis Rodolphe Lemieux MM, 22nd (French Canadian) Battalion, August 29th 1918

INDIAN – TRIBE 6 NATIONS. DIED FOR HONOUR OF EMPIRE.
EVER REMEMBERED BY WIFE AND CHILDREN.
Sapper Lewis Wilson, Canadian Engineers, August 31st 1918 (age 31)

AND FAITH AND HOPE AND LOVE SHALL GREET THE MORNING LIGHT.
Private Douglas Towell, 72nd Battalion, September 1st 1918 (age 21)

GO YE, TEACH THE GOSPEL OF JESUS & HIS LOVE, TO ALL. FREEDOM FOR ALL.
Private Walter Everard Alway Brown, 75th Battalion, September 4th 1918 (age 24)

OVER HIM NOW THE RED POPPIES GROW,
NODDING A LULLABY OF REST TO OUR DEAR BOY.
Private Paul Evan Gillespie, Canadian Army Medical Corps, September 7th 1918 (age 19)

LOVE FOLLOWS YOU WHERE YOU ROAM, LADDIE, OVER THE HILLS OF GOD.
Corporal Nelson Richardson MM, 5th Canadian Mounted Rifles, September 9th 1918 (age 20)

The male figure in an attitude of mourning alludes to the fathers left bereaved by the Great War.

3RD BATT. IN LOVING MEMORY OF CORP. FRANK PHILLIPS.
WOUNDED AND GASSED 1916. DIED SEPT. 10, 1918. AGED 22 YEARS.

HE WEARS A CROWN. I WEAR A CROSS. MOTHER
Private Charles Ramsey Ainslie, 8th Battalion, September 23rd 1918 (age 26)

IN CALIFORNIA I HEARD MY COUNTRY CALLING ME.
Private Herbert James Good, 72nd Battalion, September 28th 1918 (age 35)

ALL HE CAME TO GIVE HE GAVE.
Lieutenant Francis Langhore, 2nd Canadian Mounted Rifles, September 29th 1918 (age 25)

HE GAVE HIS LIFE THAT RIGHT MIGHT PREVAIL.
Private Cecil Harding Pick, 54th Battalion, September 30th 1918 (age 23)

A SON OF VENEZUELA WHO FOUGHT AND DIED FOR GOD'S JUSTICE ON EARTH.
Private Manuel Bermudez, 14th Battalion, October 1st 1918 (age 23)

DUTIES FAITHFULLY FULFILLED.
Nursing Sister Matilda Ethel Green, Canadian Army Nursing Service, October 9th 1918 (age 32)

WE HEAR HIM THOUGH UNSEEN AS HIS DEAR SPIRIT TREADS THE HEAVENLY PATH.
Private Herbert Davis, 28th Battalion, October 10th 1918 (age 21)

LOVE IS ETERNAL, WITHOUT BEGINNING, NOW AND FOR ALL TIME. "J'ATTENDS."
Major James Christian Lawrence Young, 1st Canadian Division Headquarters, October 13th 1918 (age 25)

3RD BATT. IN LOVING MEMORY OF PTE EDWARD PARKER.
WOUNDED AT YPRES JUNE 1916. DIED OCT. 14, 1918. AGED 28 YEARS.

WE MISS OUR BOY BUT IT HELPS TO KNOW THAT HE FELL FACING BRITAIN'S FOE.
Private Walter Newman, 43rd Battalion, October 28th 1918 (age 18)

ALL SERVICE RANKS THE SAME WITH GOD.
Private Clarence Verner Train, 54th Battalion, October 29th 1918 (age 21)

The Ploegsteert Memorial records the names of 11,447 missing British and South African soldiers who fell south of the Ypres salient and north of Fromelles between 1914 and 1918. It was dedicated in 1931, three years after the Menin Gate.

Translated from the warfare of the world into the peace of God.

BELOVED DAUGHTER & SISTER WHO ANSWERED THE CALL OF COUNTRY AND HONOR.
Nursing Sister Victoria Belle Hennan, Canadian Army Medical Corps, October 23rd 1918 (age 31)

OUR FAMILY CIRCLE IS BROKEN. OUR DEAR BOY.
Sergeant Wellesley McCann, 44th Battalion, November 1st 1918 (age 29)

IN MEMORY OF MY BELOVED BOY. GASSED AUG. 29 1918.
Gunner John McCleary, Canadian Field Artillery, November 22nd 1918 (age 22)

A FRENCH CANADIAN'S LOVE OF MOTHER AND CANADA.
Gunner Alexander Wilfred Laurier Chenette, Canadian Field Artillery, December 5th 1918 (age 23)

SLEEP ON, DEAR SON, AND TAKE THY REST. IT'S GOD'S WILL, WHO SHALL MURMUR.
Sapper John Charles Badcock, Canadian Engineers, January 22nd 1919 (age 30)

6TH BATT. 1ST DIV. IN LOVING MEMORY OF LIEUT. H.C. CHEDZEY.
WOUNDED AT HILL 70 AUG. 16, 1917. DIED JAN. 26, 1919. AGED 30 YEARS.

FOR GOD IS NOT UNRIGHTEOUS TO FORGET YOUR WORK AND LABOUR OF LOVE. HEB. 6-10
Private John Goff, Canadian Machine Gun Corps, January 31st 1919 (age 24)

FOLD UP THE TENT. A VOICE IS CALLING ME TO REST, TO REST.
Sapper Nicholas Ilitch Popoff, Canadian Railway Troops, February 9th 1919 (age 28)

92ND BATT. IN LOVING MEMORY OF PTE. JOHN FINN.
GASSED IN THE SOMME – 1918. DIED SEPT. 18 1919. AGED 24 YEARS

IN LOVING MEMORY OF PTE. JOHN W. LAWRENCE.
DIED IN WESTERN HOSPITAL FEB. 8 1920. AGED 37 YEARS.

R.C.R. C.E.C. IN LOVING MEMORY OF SAP. J (PERCY) BROWN.
DIED AT DAVISVILLE HOSPITAL APRIL 15 1920. AGED 23 YEARS.

32ND BATT. IN LOVING MEMORY OF PTE. HUGH QUINN. WOUNDED 1917.
DIED DAVISVILLE HOSP. JULY 24 1920. AGED 36 YEARS.

Suggestions for Further Reading

This is not an academic book and is not intended for an academic readership, though it may be of some use or interest to scholars working on the First World War. I have therefore not burdened the text with footnotes or a scholarly apparatus, but I wish here to acknowledge my debt to a number of works and to offer a list of books and articles which readers may wish to consult.

The study of the epitaphs begins with the story of the Imperial (now Commonwealth) War Graves Commission, well covered by Philip Longworth, *The Unending Vigil: A History of the Commonwealth War Graves Commission* (first published in 1967; reprinted: Barnsley, South Yorkshire: Pen and Sword Books, 2003), and David Crane's *Empires of the Dead: How One Man's Vision Led to the Creation of WW1's War Graves* (London: William Collin, 2013). Collections and discussions of Great War epitaphs may be found in John Laffin's pioneering *We Will Remember Them: AIF Epitaphs of World War 1* (Kenthurst, Australia: Kangaroo Press, 1995); Trefor Jones, *On Fame's Eternal Camping Ground: A Study of First World War Epitaphs in the British Cemeteries of the Western Front* (Trowbridge, Wiltshire: Cromwell Press, 2007); Sarah Wearne, *Epitaphs of the Great War: The Somme* (London: Unicorn Publishing Group, 2016); and my own "Time but the impression deeper makes: Approaches to Canadian epitaphs of the Great War," *Canadian Military History* 22, no. 2 (Summer 2013), and *Words of Valediction and Remembrance: Canadian Epitaphs of the Second World War* (St. Catharines, Ont.: Vanwell Press, 2008).

Readers interested in the details of the soldiers whose epitaphs are given in this book should go to the Canadian Virtual War Memorial site, at www.veterans.gc.ca/eng/remembrance/memorials/canadian-virtual-war-memorial; photographs of their headstones are available (thanks to Steve Douglas and hundreds of volunteers) at mapleleaflegacy.ca. For further background on epitaphs, these books are recommended: Karl Guthke, *Epitaph Culture in the West: Variations on a Theme in Cultural History* (Lewiston-Queenston-Lampeter: Edwin Mellen Press, 2003); Richmond

Lattimore, *Themes in Greek and Latin Epitaphs* (Urbana: University of Illinois Press, 1962), and Joshua Scodel, *The English Poetic Epitaph: Commemoration and Conflict from Jonson to Wordsworth* (Ithaca NY: Cornell University Press, 1991).

On the effects of the Great War and the response to the collective grief, Jay Winter's *Sites of Memory, Sites of Mourning: The Great War in European Cultural History* (Cambridge: Cambridge University Press, 1995) remains indispensable; in the closer Canadian context, yet relevant to all the English-speaking Dominions, two works by Jonathan Vance, *Death So Noble: Memory, Meaning, and the First World War* (Vancouver: UBC Press, 1997), and "Remembering Armageddon," in David Mackenzie, ed., *Canada and the First World War: Essays in Honour of Robert Craig Brown* (Toronto: University of Toronto Press, 2005), 409–33, are the field's foundation texts. See also Alan R. Young, "'We throw the torch': Canadian Memorials of the Great War and the Mythology of Heroic Sacrifice," *Journal of Canadian Studies* 24, no. 4 (Winter 1989–90), 5–28. The literary heritage in Canada of the Great War is explored in Jonathan Vance's "Battle verse: Poetry and nationalism after Vimy Ridge," in *Vimy Ridge: A Canadian Reassessment* (ed. Geoffrey Hayes, Andrew Iarocci, and Mike Bechthold (Waterloo, Ont.: Wilfrid Laurier University Press, 2007), 265–77, and Joel Baetz, ed., *Canadian Poetry from World War I: An Anthology* (Toronto: Oxford University Press, 2009).

On the battles fought by the Canadian Corps and the experience of its soldiers, I have relied primarily on Tim Cook's two-volume history *At The Sharp End: Canadians Fighting the Great War 1914–1916* and *Shock Troops: Canadians Fighting the Great War 1917–1918* (Toronto: Viking Canada, 2007 and 2008), and Desmond Morton's *When Your Number's Up: The Canadian Soldier in the First World War* (Toronto: Random House, 1993). Readers interested in visiting the battlefields where Canadians fought in the First World War should turn to the Battlefield Europe series, which has excellent guides for the Somme battles, Flanders, and Vimy Ridge; Canadian readers will also wish to consult *Canadian Battlefields of the First World War: A Visitor's Guide,* by Terry Copp, Nick Lachance, Caitlin McWilliams, and Matt Symes, edited by Mark Humphries, available from Wilfrid Laurier University Press.

Acknowledgements

It is a pleasure to thank the people who supported the writing of this book and helped it into print. My thanks go first to Ryan Gearing at Unicorn Publishing Group for his interest in a book on Canadian epitaphs of the Great War and for his assistance in laying out a path to publication; Ryan also deserves thanks for putting the task of designing an unusual book in the capable, creative hands of Felicity Price-Smith, to whom I express my gratitude for her fine work. I am grateful to Terry Copp for providing a foreword and wish to take this opportunity to note my admiration not only for his work but also for the encouragement he has offered to so many students and colleagues over the years – truly a fine and generous scholar. A special thanks goes to my friend John Rosolak for serving as a one-man general reader and offering some very useful suggestions on the chapters I ran by him. This is also the place to thank Susan Ross and her colleagues at the Canadian War Museum in Ottawa for their efficiency and courtesy in arranging for the publication of the war art used in this book. To my collaborator Steve Douglas, I wish to say how glad I was that we could put text and image together in a book about a subject deeply meaningful to us both. Many Canadians will know Steve as the founder of the Maple Leaf Legacy Project, a labour of love and a great service that has made photographs of every Canadian grave from the World Wars and other conflicts available online; I hope that this book will introduce readers to Steve's talents as a photographer and lead travellers to his remarkable bookshop in Ieper near the Menin Gate.

Finally, my affectionate thanks to my wife Sylvia who enabled me to write this book by taking on a larger share of the load at home. She has also been a discerning reader whose thoughts and comments are always on the mark. To her, and to my precious children Sarah and Colin, I convey my love and gratitude, and look forward to a return to normal now that this book is done.

Eric McGeer, Toronto, Canada, March 2017

Acknowledgements

My sincere thanks to my friend Eric McGeer for his dedication and hard work on this project and for his talent as a writer. I would like to echo Eric's words, above, in thanking Ryan and Felicity, at Unicorn, for their patience and persistence in helping us get this book published. Thanks, too, to my parents for getting me started with my love and fascination of photography when I was thirteen. The idea of capturing a moment in time and preserving it still fascinates me today.

No one visiting the Commonwealth cemeteries can fail to admire the work of the CWGC staff and gardeners. Their sure touch in creating and maintaining places of such beauty and tranquility makes the photographer's task an absorbing yet simple exercise.

Finally, I wish to dedicate my part of this book to my dear friend, Tanya, whose selfless dedication to her son, Zac, is awesome to see and an inspiration to me. Thank you for being a part of my life.

Steve Douglas, Ypres, Belgium, March 2017

Chapter-Opener Images

Copyright Acknowledgements

List of Abbreviations

DCM	Distinguished Conduct Medal	DSM	Distinguished Service Medal	DSO	Distinguished Service Order
MC	Military Cross	MM	Military Medal	VC	Victoria Cross